STERLING BIOGRAPHIES

MARTIN LUTHER KING, JR.

A Dream of Hope

Alice Fleming

STERLING

New York / London
www.sterlingpublishing.com/kids

STERLING and the distinctive Sterling logo are registered trademarks of
Sterling Publishing Co., Inc.

Library of Congress Cataloging-in-Publication Data

Fleming, Alice Mulcahey, 1928-
    Martin Luther King, Jr. : the voice of civil rights / Alice Fleming.
        p. cm. -- (Sterling biographies)
    Includes bibliographical references and index.
    ISBN 978-1-4027-4439-6
    1. King, Martin Luther, Jr., 1929-1968--Juvenile literature. 2. African Americans--Biography--
Juvenile literature. 3. Civil rights workers--United States--Biography--Juvenile literature. 4.
Baptists--United States--Clergy--Biography--Juvenile literature. 5. African Americans--Civil
rights--History--20th century--Juvenile literature. I. Title.

E185.97.K5F58 2008
323.092--dc22
[B]

                                                    2007019271

10 9 8 7 6 5
03/13

Published by Sterling Publishing Co., Inc.
387 Park Avenue South, New York, NY 10016
© 2008 by Alice Fleming
All Primary Material Copyright © Dr. Martin Luther King, Jr.
All Primary Material Copyright © renewed Coretta Scott King
and the Heirs to the Estate of Dr. Martin Luther King, Jr.
All reprinted by permission of Writer's House, LLC
Distributed in Canada by Sterling Publishing
c/o Canadian Manda Group, 165 Dufferin Street
Toronto, Ontario, Canada M6K 3H6
Distributed in the United Kingdom by GMC Distribution Services
Castle Place, 166 High Street, Lewes, East Sussex, England BN7 1XU
Distributed in Australia by Capricorn Link (Australia) Pty. Ltd.
P.O. Box 704, Windsor, NSW 2756, Australia

Printed in China
All rights reserved

Sterling ISBN 978-1-4027-4439-6 (paperback)

Sterling ISBN 978-1-4027-5803-4 (hardcover)

Designed by Frieda Christofides for SimonSays Design!
Image research by Susan Schader

For information about custom editions, special sales, premium and
corporate purchases, please contact Sterling Special Sales
Department at 800-805-5489 or specialsales@sterlingpublishing.com.

Contents

Events in the Life of Martin Luther King, Jr.

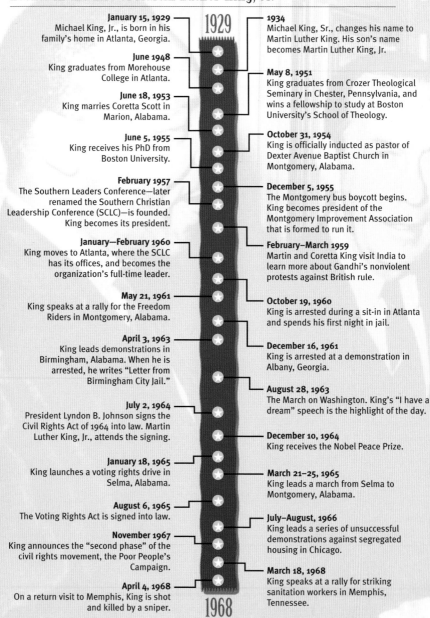

January 15, 1929
Michael King, Jr., is born in his family's home in Atlanta, Georgia.

1934
Michael King, Sr., changes his name to Martin Luther King. His son's name becomes Martin Luther King, Jr.

June 1948
King graduates from Morehouse College in Atlanta.

May 8, 1951
King graduates from Crozer Theological Seminary in Chester, Pennsylvania, and wins a fellowship to study at Boston University's School of Theology.

June 18, 1953
King marries Coretta Scott in Marion, Alabama.

October 31, 1954
King is officially inducted as pastor of Dexter Avenue Baptist Church in Montgomery, Alabama.

June 5, 1955
King receives his PhD from Boston University.

December 5, 1955
The Montgomery bus boycott begins. King becomes president of the Montgomery Improvement Association that is formed to run it.

February 1957
The Southern Leaders Conference—later renamed the Southern Christian Leadership Conference (SCLC)—is founded. King becomes its president.

February–March 1959
Martin and Coretta King visit India to learn more about Gandhi's nonviolent protests against British rule.

January–February 1960
King moves to Atlanta, where the SCLC has its offices, and becomes the organization's full-time leader.

October 19, 1960
King is arrested during a sit-in in Atlanta and spends his first night in jail.

May 21, 1961
King speaks at a rally for the Freedom Riders in Montgomery, Alabama.

December 16, 1961
King is arrested at a demonstration in Albany, Georgia.

April 3, 1963
King leads demonstrations in Birmingham, Alabama. When he is arrested, he writes "Letter from Birmingham City Jail."

August 28, 1963
The March on Washington. King's "I have a dream" speech is the highlight of the day.

July 2, 1964
President Lyndon B. Johnson signs the Civil Rights Act of 1964 into law. Martin Luther King, Jr., attends the signing.

December 10, 1964
King receives the Nobel Peace Prize.

January 18, 1965
King launches a voting rights drive in Selma, Alabama.

March 21–25, 1965
King leads a march from Selma to Montgomery, Alabama.

August 6, 1965
The Voting Rights Act is signed into law.

July–August, 1966
King leads a series of unsuccessful demonstrations against segregated housing in Chicago.

November 1967
King announces the "second phase" of the civil rights movement, the Poor People's Campaign.

March 18, 1968
King speaks at a rally for striking sanitation workers in Memphis, Tennessee.

April 4, 1968
On a return visit to Memphis, King is shot and killed by a sniper.

1929

1968

Opening the Door to Opportunity

I may be crucified for my beliefs, and if I am,
you can say, "He died to make men free."

There was a time, not so very long ago, when there were few, if any, African Americans in the halls of Congress, on the campuses of elite universities, or in the ranks of corporate executives. These days—thanks to a single-minded man named Martin Luther King, Jr.—blacks are no longer a rarity in such places.

King was the pastor of a small Baptist church in Montgomery, Alabama, when he was chosen to lead a black **boycott** of the city's bus lines. The boycott started the civil rights movement, and King became its driving force. His nonviolent campaign of marches and demonstrations and his brilliance as a public speaker rescued the nation's African Americans from decades of oppression, and led to sweeping new laws that finally gave them the rights—and the opportunities—they deserved.

CHAPTER 1

Sweet Auburn

You just wait and see. When I grow up I'm going to get me some big words.

Martin Luther King, Jr., was raised in a family where religion played a major role. His father, Michael King, Sr., grew up poor and uneducated in rural Georgia. At the age of fifteen he left home and went to Atlanta. When he had earned enough money and completed enough schooling, he enrolled at Morehouse College to study for the ministry.

By then Mike had fallen in love with Alberta Christine Williams, whose father, the Reverend A. D. Williams, was pastor of Ebenezer Baptist Church, one of the largest African American churches in Atlanta. Mike and Alberta were married in 1926 and moved into the second floor of the Williamses' house on Auburn Avenue in one of Atlanta's busiest black neighborhoods.

Martin Luther King, Jr., spent a lot of his childhood time at Ebenezer Baptist Church, where both his grandfather and father were pastors. The church has been managed by the National Park Service as a historic site since 1999.

The young couple lost no time in starting a family. Their first child, a daughter, Willie Christine, was born in 1927. Less than two years later, on January 15, 1929, they had a son, Michael, Jr. In 1930, a second son, Alfred Daniel (A. D. for short), was born. The year after A. D.'s birth, Alberta's father, the Reverend A. D. Williams, died and Mike King, who had been serving as assistant pastor of Ebenezer Baptist Church, took his father-in-law's place as pastor.

For some reason—possibly because it sounded more dignified—Mike decided to change his name to Martin Luther King in honor of the German reformer who founded Protestantism. Young Michael, who was five at the time, became Martin Luther King, Jr.—M. L. for short.

Racial Barriers

M. L. grew up at a time when a distressing number of Americans believed that white people were superior to blacks. This belief was particularly strong in the South, where Jim Crow laws kept black people strictly segregated, or apart, from whites. There were separate accommodations—such as schools and restaurants—for whites and for blacks. The arrangement should

A 1940 photograph shows a segregated restaurant in Durham, North Carolina. The restaurant has separate entrances marked "White" and "Colored."

have been—but wasn't—illegal. Some years earlier, the Supreme Court had ruled that separate facilities for the two races did not violate the U.S. Constitution as long as the facilities for blacks were equal to those for whites—which, of course, they never were.

M. L. had his first encounter with **segregation** when he was six years old. His favorite playmate was a white boy whose father owned a store across the street from the Kings' home. When it was time to start school, M. L. was dismayed to discover that he and his friend would be attending different schools. The other boy's school was for whites; M. L.'s school was for blacks. To make matters worse, the boy's parents told M. L. that the two boys could no longer play together. When M. L. asked why, they said, "Because we are white and you are colored."

That evening, M. L. told his parents what had happened. They responded by giving him a brief history of race relations in the United States. They explained how the first Negroes—as African Americans were called in those days—had come to America as slaves and how, even after slavery ended, whites continued to look down on blacks. They were willing to hire them as servants or laborers, but otherwise they wanted nothing to do with them. That was why M. L. and his white friend would be attending separate schools and why M. L.'s school would almost certainly be inferior to his friend's.

The information came as a shock to M. L. Thus far in his life, he had met very few white people. He had no idea how any of them felt about blacks. As the children of the Reverend Martin Luther King, he and his siblings were treated with respect by everyone in "Sweet Auburn," as the area around Auburn Avenue was called. M. L. found it hard to believe that they would not be welcome in other parts of town.

Jim Crow Laws

After the Civil War, the nation adopted three **amendments** to the U.S. **Constitution**. The Thirteenth Amendment freed the slaves; the Fourteenth made blacks citizens of the United States; and the Fifteenth gave black males the right to vote.

In theory, African Americans should have enjoyed the same rights as white people. In reality, this was not the case.

Beginning in the 1870s, Southern states and states close to the South passed Jim Crow laws that required blacks to be segregated from whites in schools, restaurants, buses, and anywhere else the two races might mingle. The laws were named after a character in the **minstrel shows** shows that were popular in the nineteenth century.

The "separate but equal" doctrine is depicted in this 1913 cartoon that shows white passengers comfortably seated in the front of the plane, while blacks trail behind in an airborne version of a Jim Crow car.

In 1892, a black man named Homer Plessy was arrested in New Orleans for violating the Jim Crow laws by sitting in a white-only railroad car. Plessy challenged his arrest, arguing that the Fourteenth Amendment to the Constitution guaranteed blacks equal treatment under the law.

The case, *Plessy v. Ferguson*, eventually went to the Supreme Court where the justices ruled that segregation was permissible under the Fourteenth Amendment as long as the accommodations for blacks were equal to those for whites. The ruling established the seperate but equal doctrine, which remained in effect for the next fifty-eight years.

Family Relations

Like his namesake, the sixteenth-century clergyman Martin Luther, the Reverend King was a man with strong convictions. He detested segregation and rarely hesitated to make his feelings known. One day, M. L. and his father were shopping for shoes in a downtown store. A sales clerk informed them that if they wanted to get waited on, they would have to move to the back of the store.

"We'll either buy shoes sitting here or we won't buy shoes at all," Martin King declared. When the clerk walked away without helping them, Martin, with M. L. in tow, marched out of the store.

Unfortunately, Martin Luther King, Sr., was equally aggressive at home. He expected all of his children to obey his every wish. When they didn't, he disciplined them with a leather strap. M. L. endured his father's punishments in silence. Although his face was often covered with tears, he never uttered a sound. After the beatings, M. L. would turn to his grandmother for comfort. A gentle, kindly woman, Mama Williams lived with the Kings after her husband's death.

M. L. was a small, slightly pudgy, and somewhat solemn child. He liked to ride his bicycle, fly model airplanes, and play ball with the other boys in the neighborhood. He also had a quick temper, which occasionally led to fistfights. His brother, A. D., had an equally short fuse. The two boys sometimes got into arguments, as brothers often do. One of their disputes ended with A. D. bashing M. L. with a baseball bat. On another occasion, M. L. hit A. D. in the head with a telephone and knocked him out.

As the children and grandchildren of ministers, the King children were taught to believe in God and respect His teachings. There were family prayers in the morning and evening, and the greater part of every Sunday was spent in church. By the time M. L. was five, he could recite long passages from the Bible by heart and knew the words to dozens of hymns. He often sang them at church events with Mama Williams accompanying him on the piano.

Language held a special fascination for M. L. One of the most exciting experiences of his childhood was listening to a visiting preacher at Ebenezer Baptist Church. The man used long words that rolled off his tongue with the rhythm and power of great poetry.

The interior of Ebenezer Baptist Church, at 407 Auburn Avenue, in northeast Atlanta. The church, which was founded in 1868, had several homes before moving to its present site in 1922.

"You just wait and see," M. L. told his parents. "When I grow up I'm going to get me some big words."

In many ways, M. L. was closer to his grandmother than he was to his parents. When Mama died unexpectedly in the spring of 1941, M. L. was so distraught that he rushed upstairs and jumped out a second-story window. Although badly bruised, he was not seriously hurt. It took a long time for M. L.'s grief to subside, mainly because he felt guilty about Mama's death. He was convinced that God had punished him for sneaking off that day without permission to watch a parade.

Although M. L. never forgot his grandmother, he eventually came to realize that her death was not his fault. His sorrow was further eased when the Kings moved out of the house on Auburn Avenue, where Mama had been such a presence, and into a newer house a few blocks away. A year later, there was another change in M. L.'s life. He graduated from eighth grade and started high school.

CHAPTER 2

School Days

That night will never leave my memory. It was the angriest I have ever been in my life.

M. L. attended Booker T. Washington High School. He began to notice girls, learned the latest dance steps, and became known for his stylish clothes. Although he liked to have a good time, he also had a serious side. At home, he could often be found sitting quietly in his room reading a book.

M. L.'s serious side also became apparent in school. Although his marks were never more than average, he excelled at public speaking. His mellow voice and ease with words made him the star of Booker T. Washington's debating team. In his junior year, he entered an **oratorical**

M. L. and his high school teacher, Mrs. Bradley, probably rode on a segregated bus like the one pictured here, which had the front section marked "Whites" and the back marked "Negroes" or "Colored." In many places, blacks were required to pay their fare at the front of the bus, then get off and re-enter through the rear door.

contest sponsored by the Negro Elks Club in Dublin, Georgia, about a hundred miles from Atlanta. M. L. gave a speech on "The Negro and the Constitution" for which he was awarded first prize.

After the contest ended, M. L. and the teacher who had accompanied him to Dublin, Mrs. Bradley, took the bus back to Atlanta. They had gone only a few miles when the driver stopped to pick up some white passengers. All the seats were taken, so the driver ordered M. L. and his teacher to stand up and let the whites sit down. When they did not obey instantly, the bus driver made an insulting remark about Negroes.

M. L. was so infuriated that he refused to budge. Mrs. Bradley whispered to him to do as the man said, otherwise he would be breaking the law. M. L. obeyed and he and Mrs. Bradley stood for the rest of the trip.

Although M. L. had been living with segregation for his entire life, he had never experienced it so directly. "That night will never leave my mind," he said later. "It was the angriest I have ever been in my life."

Further Education

Martin King and the Reverend A. D. Williams had both graduated from Morehouse College. The all-male school, which was founded in 1867 to educate newly freed slaves, was the college of choice for the sons of Atlanta's African American middle class. M. L. planned to go there, too.

In M. L.'s junior year at Booker T. Washington, Morehouse announced that it would accept any high school juniors who could pass its entrance exam. Most of its students had abandoned their studies to fight in World War II and the college was desperate to fill its classrooms. M. L. passed the exam and, in 1944, he became a freshman at Morehouse. He was fifteen years old.

As a college student, M. L. continued to enjoy parties and dances. He was not an ambitious student, and he had only a vague idea of what he wanted to do when he graduated. All he knew was that he wanted to help African Americans.

All he knew was that he wanted to help African Americans.

On one of his summer vacations from Morehouse, M. L. got a look at what life could be like without segregation. He took a job on a tobacco farm near Hartford, Connecticut. There were no Jim Crow laws in the North, so when M. L. and his friends went into Hartford on weekends, they could eat in any restaurant they pleased and see a movie without having to sit in the "colored" section of the balcony.

The trip back home to Atlanta was a cruel reminder of how different things were in the South. At the beginning of his journey, M. L. sat in the same car as the other passengers. When he arrived in Washington, D.C., and changed to the train to Atlanta, however, he had to move to the car set aside for blacks. When he went to the dining car, a waiter led him to a rear table and drew a curtain around it so the white patrons wouldn't see him.

Choosing a Career

M. L. knew that many black clergymen considered fighting for their people an important part of their job. His grandfather, the Reverend A. D. Williams, had been one of the founders of the Atlanta chapter of the National Association for the Advancement of Colored People (NAACP). The Reverend Martin Luther King, Sr., was an active member of the chapter.

Although becoming a minister would fulfill M. L.'s desire to help his fellow blacks, the calling did not appeal to him. After spending so many Sundays in his father's church, M. L. had lost his enthusiasm for religion.

When Martin King, Sr., preached a sermon, his congregation swayed and clapped their hands. When he said something they particularly liked, they would shout, "Amen!" or "That's right!" or "Tell it, Reverend!" M. L. disliked these unrestrained displays of emotion. He thought they robbed religion of its dignity.

The president of Morehouse College, Dr. Benjamin Mays, became M. L.'s friend and mentor. Mays was also a minister, but his sermons appealed to his listeners' intellect rather than their emotions. When Mays talked about racism, for instance, his approach was thoughtful and practical rather than angry. Under Mays's influence, M. L. began to see that he could be a minister and still be a serious thinker. Thoughtful sermons did not inspire emotional outbursts.

Dr. Benjamin Mays, a native of South Carolina and the son of slaves, earned a PhD from the University of Chicago and was president of Morehouse College from 1940 to 1967. Mays's thoughtful sermons inspired M. L. to become a preacher.

The National Association for the Advancement of Colored People

The National Association for the Advancement of Colored People (NAACP) is the oldest civil rights organization in the United States. It was founded in 1910 in the aftermath of a race riot in Springfield, Illinois, that resulted in the **lynching** of two black men. Their deaths horrified many Northern whites and prompted a New York woman, Mary White Ovington, to organize an interracial association aimed at ending segregation and discrimination and achieving equal citizenship rights for Negroes.

A National Association for the Advancement of Colored People (NAACP) office in Detroit, Michigan, during the 1940s. The organization's first governing board consisted of seven whites and one black. Today, the leadership is almost exclusively black.

In the beginning, the association was dominated by whites. Then, in 1916, the NAACP hired lawyer, author, and educator James Weldon Johnson as its first black executive secretary. He recruited large numbers of black members and set up branches in Southern cities and towns. By 1920, most of the NAACP chapters and almost half its members were in the South.

The NAACP publicized the evils of Jim Crow laws and conducted a successful crusade against lynching. The organization achieved its most important victory in 1954 when the NAACP Legal Defense and Education Fund persuaded the United States Supreme Court to overturn *Plessy v. Ferguson* and declare the "separate but equal" doctrine illegal.

When M. L. told his father that he had decided to become a minister, Martin King invited him to preach a trial sermon at Ebenezer Baptist Church. M. L. proved to be a good preacher, and the congregation showered him with praise. A few weeks later, M. L. was back in the pulpit, but this time it was to extend an apology. Baptists disapproved of dancing, especially by their ministers, so when Martin King, Sr., discovered that M. L. had gone to a dance, he made his son apologize to the entire congregation at the next Sunday service.

Seminary Life

After his graduation from Morehouse, M. L. attended Crozer Theological Seminary in Chester, Pennsylvania. Though Crozer had an enrollment of around one hundred, there were very few black students, only six in M. L.'s class. For the first time in his life, M. L. was living among whites. His father had warned him to expect trouble, but in his three years at Crozer he encountered only one instance of prejudice.

A notorious **bigot,** a student from North Carolina, appeared at M. L.'s door one day carrying a pistol and threatening to shoot him. The student's room had been trashed, and he was convinced—mistakenly—that M. L. had done it. M. L. remained calm. He talked to the man quietly and kept him at bay until several other students came to the rescue. The case was brought before the student government. They could have expelled the North Carolinian, but M. L. refused to press charges. The white student apologized, and the two men eventually became friends.

The Power of Love and Truth

One Sunday while Martin was studying at Crozer, he went to Philadelphia to hear a lecture by Dr. Mordecai W. Johnson, the

Mohandas K. Gandhi (1869–1948)

Mohandas K.—Mahatma—Gandhi, shown in a c. 1931 photograph, began his nonviolent protests against India's colonial government in 1919. King discovered that Gandhi's peaceful demonstrations could be used to good effect in the American South.

Mohandas K. Gandhi was born in India in 1869, when the country was a British colony. In 1893, he moved to Durban, South Africa, where he gained equal rights for South Africa's Indians by protesting discrimination through general **strikes** and marches conducted in a peaceful manner. Gandhi's success in South Africa made him a hero in his native country. When he returned to India in 1915, he was given the title Mahatma, or Great Soul. He began carrying a bamboo staff and wearing a dhoti, a native costume consisting of a loincloth and shawl, to symbolize his rejection of material things.

Gandhi spent the next three decades pressuring Great Britain to give Indians a role in the colonial government. He resorted to the same tactics that had worked so well in South Africa: strikes, marches, **fasts**-until-death, and a willingness to be jailed for his beliefs. At the end of World War II, England finally granted independence to India. There was a violent clash between the country's two major religious groups, the Hindus and the Moslems. In 1948, the Mahatma was shot and killed while conducting a prayer meeting for peace. His assailant was a Hindu fanatic who objected to Gandhi's tolerance toward Moslems.

president of Howard University in Washington, D.C. Johnson had recently returned from India, and his lecture was devoted to the ideas of the Indian political and spiritual leader, Mohandas K. Gandhi. Gandhi's nonviolent marches and demonstrations against British rule helped India win her independence from Great Britain in 1947.

Johnson explained how Gandhi had used an approach he called Soul Force—the power of love and truth—to bring about social change. Johnson believed that the approach Gandhi and his followers had used in India could be used against racial discrimination in the United States. King found Johnson's statements "so profound and electrifying" that he went out and bought a half-dozen books on Gandhi's life and works.

M. L. graduated from Crozer in 1951. He ranked first in his class and gave the **valedictory** address at graduation. He also won a scholarship to study for his **doctorate** at the graduate school of his choice.

M. L. spent the summer preaching at Ebenezer Baptist Church so Daddy King—the name Martin King, Sr., used now that there were two Reverend Kings in the family—could take a vacation. In September, M. L. set out for Massachusetts in the new green Chevrolet his father had given him for graduation. He was going to study at Boston University's School of Theology.

CHAPTER 3

A Mind of His Own

I'm going to get my doctorate and then I'm going to marry Coretta.

Martin began his studies at Boston University in the fall of 1951. He found the graduate courses in religion and **philosophy** more challenging than the courses he had taken at Crozer. He analyzed the views of the world's great thinkers and explored such questions as the conflict between good and evil and God's role in the personal lives of human beings.

In the midst of wrestling with these large ideas, Martin managed to have a busy social life. Although he had no trouble finding young women to take to parties, he was tired of casual friendships. He wanted to find someone he could marry. The wife of one of his friends gave him the phone numbers of two young women he might like. One was Coretta Scott, an Alabama girl who was studying singing at the New England Conservatory of Music.

Courtship and Marriage

One night in 1952, Martin called Coretta and asked if they could meet. Although she was hesitant about going out with a Baptist preacher—all the ones she had met were stuffy and self-important—Coretta agreed to have lunch with him. The lunch went well, but Coretta was taken by surprise when Martin told her that she had all four qualities he wanted in a wife: character, intelligence, personality, and beauty. Coretta thought it was much too soon to be talking about marriage. They had only just met. Still, she liked him enough to see him again.

Coretta and Martin were soon spending quite a bit of time together. They went to concerts at Boston's Symphony Hall and took long walks around the city. Martin continued to talk about marriage, but Coretta kept putting him off. He had already told her he wanted a wife who would be a full-time homemaker and a partner in his ministry. Coretta had other plans. She wanted to become a concert singer. Martin persisted, and in the end Coretta decided that she loved him enough to give up her dream.

Daddy King was sorry to hear that his son was serious about Coretta Scott. Daddy expected him to marry a girl from Atlanta whom he had already picked out. When Martin insisted that

he was going to choose his own wife, Daddy King accused him of neglecting his studies by spending too much time with Coretta. Martin stood his ground. He assured Daddy King that he was in no danger of flunking out of graduate school.

"I'm going to get my doctorate," he announced firmly, "and then I'm going to marry Coretta." Daddy King backed down and gave his blessing to the match.

Martin and Coretta were married on the lawn of Coretta's home in Marion, Alabama, on June 18, 1953. Daddy King performed

Martin and Coretta King in their wedding portrait, June 18, 1953. Coretta insisted that Martin's father, who officiated at the ceremony, omit the promise to obey her husband from their wedding vows.

the ceremony. At that time, hotels and motels in Alabama did not rent rooms to Negroes, so the newlyweds had to spend their wedding night in the guest quarters of a funeral home that was owned by a friend of the Scotts.

Back in Boston, Martin and Coretta moved into a small apartment near the New England Conservatory. Martin had already completed the courses he needed for his degree and was writing his **dissertation**—the final step in the long process of becoming a PhD. Coretta had one more year of school. After she graduated, there would be no need for the Kings to remain in Boston. Martin could find a job and finish his dissertation in his free time.

One of his advisers at Boston University thought Martin had the makings of a serious scholar and suggested that he become a professor. His old friend, Dr. Benjamin Mays, offered him a position at Morehouse College. Although Martin was tempted by the offer, most of the educators he admired, including Mays, had served as ministers before joining the academic world. He decided to pursue the same path.

Dexter Avenue Baptist Church

Martin applied for the position of pastor at several churches. The one that was most interested in hiring him was Dexter Avenue Baptist Church in Montgomery, Alabama. Its membership was composed mainly of educated blacks—doctors, lawyers, nurses, and professors at Alabama State College—who would appreciate a learned minister.

Martin's decision to serve at Dexter Avenue Baptist Church disappointed Daddy King. He had asked Martin to become his assistant at Ebenezer Baptist, with the hope that when he retired, Martin would take over as pastor. Daddy could not understand

Coretta Scott King (1927–2006)

Coretta Scott was born in Marion, Alabama, on April 27, 1927. Her father, Obadiah Leonard Scott, earned a reasonably good living as a farmer. Both he and her mother, Bernice McMurry Scott, encouraged their children to do well in school.

In 1945, Coretta followed her older sister, Edyth, to Antioch College in Yellow Springs, Ohio. Coretta earned a degree in music and elementary education. In 1951, she won a grant to study voice at the New England Conservatory of Music in Boston, Massachusetts. It was there that she met and fell in love with Martin Luther King, Jr.

After their marriage, Coretta devoted most of her time to raising their four children. She made occasional speeches and performed "freedom concerts" to support the work of the Southern Christian Leadership Conference. Coretta Scott King died at the age of seventy-eight in 2006.

Coretta, shown with her children in this 1964 photograph, often played the piano and led her children in song. When Martin was at home, he would add his rich baritone voice to the family chorus.

why Martin turned him down. But Martin did not want to live in his father's shadow. In his career, just as in his marriage, he intended to go his own way.

Martin gave his first sermon at Dexter in May of 1954. Two weeks later, the Supreme Court handed down its landmark decision in *Brown v. Board of Education of Topeka*. The ruling against school segregation produced little excitement among African Americans. The government had a long history of broken promises. This decision might be just one more.

Dexter Avenue Baptist Church was founded in 1879. Its first minister, a former slave named Charles Octavius Boothe, described its black members as "people of money and refinement."

Learning to be a Preacher

In the fall of 1954, Martin and Coretta King moved into Dexter's white frame parsonage, and King took up his duties as pastor. He officiated at weddings, christenings, and funerals and counseled church members who came to him with their problems.

The better part of the twenty-five-year-old minister's week, however, was devoted to preparing his Sunday sermons. They were scholarly orations studded with quotations from poets, philosophers, and religious thinkers. Although he wrote them out in advance, he delivered them from memory. His congregation was awed by his ability to preach for as long as thirty or forty minutes without any notes.

In the beginning, King's preaching style was stiff and somewhat pompous. Although his congregation congratulated him on his sermons, he sometimes wondered if he was really reaching them. He used to frown on the clapping and shouting that resounded through Ebenezer Baptist when Daddy King was in the pulpit. Now that he had a church of his own, he could see its value. African Americans needed an outlet for the anger and frustration they felt at the way they were treated by many whites.

As time went on, King gradually adopted a more freewheeling style. His sermons were still serious, but he began to talk *to* his listeners rather than *at* them. Before long, they were responding with shouts of "Amen" and "Oh, yes!" that inspired him to even greater heights of eloquence.

King's pastoral work took up so much of his time that he had to get up at 5:30 in the morning to work on his dissertation. He completed it in the spring of 1955 and received his PhD from Boston University in June. In November, the Reverend Doctor Martin Luther King, Jr., and his wife, Coretta, celebrated another milestone: Their first child, Yolanda, was born.

The Reverend Martin Luther King, Jr., preaching at Ebenezer Baptist Church in 1967. He eventually developed a preaching style that would fire up his congregation.

Brown v. Board of Education of Topeka

The Supreme Court decision in *Brown v. Board of Education of Topeka* was issued on May 17, 1954. The case was argued by black lawyers working for the NAACP. Their strategy was to focus on the "separate but equal" ruling as it applied to a single issue: segregated schools.

The NAACP lawyers found five cases that demonstrated the inequalities of all-black schools. All five went to the Supreme Court, where they were reviewed under a single title, *Brown v. Board of Education of Topeka*.

It took several months for the Supreme Court to announce its decision. Chief Justice Earl Warren read it aloud. "We conclude unanimously," he declared, "that in the field of public education, the doctrine of 'separate but equal' has no place. Separate educational facilities are inherently unequal."

The ruling overturned *Plessy v. Ferguson* and made segregation unconstitutional in the nation's public schools. Although it would be several years before the new law was enforced, the decision became the basis for rulings against segregation in other situations. The case was not only a historic breakthrough for African Americans, it resulted in one of the most important changes in the history of the United States.

A 1942 photograph of African American children learning to read at a segregated school in Washington, D.C. Washington was one of the first Southern cities to integrate its schools after *Brown v. Board of Education of Topeka*.

CHAPTER 4

The Miracle of Montgomery

I want it to be known . . . that we are Christian people. . . . The only weapon that we have in our hands this evening is the weapon of protest.

Martin Luther King, Jr., had been in Montgomery a little more than a year when the city became involved in a racial crisis. On Thursday, December 1, 1955, Rosa Parks, a black seamstress and civil rights activist who worked in a downtown department store, boarded a bus to go home from work. At the next stop, some white passengers got on. They all found seats except for one man. When the bus driver ordered Parks to give the man her seat, Parks

Rosa Parks being fingerprinted by a Montgomery, Alabama, police officer in February 1956. She was among the dozens of black leaders who were arrested for continuing the bus boycott.

ignored him. The driver warned her that if she didn't get up, he would call the police.

"You may do that," Parks said calmly. A few minutes later, the police arrived and arrested her.

Another of Montgomery's black residents, E. D. Nixon, had worked with Parks in the local chapter of the NAACP. Nixon wanted to use Parks's arrest to start a protest against segregation on public buses. When Parks agreed, Nixon invited Montgomery's black leaders to a meeting to decide what the next steps should be. Among the first people Nixon called were Martin Luther King, Jr., and Ralph Abernathy, the pastor of Montgomery's First Baptist Church. The two men were among the few black clergymen who were active in the NAACP and were the two most likely to approve of taking a stand against Parks's arrest.

The meeting was held on Friday evening, December 2. The leaders agreed to protest Parks's arrest by asking the city's African Americans to stay off the buses on Monday, December 5, the day of her trial. Thousands of flyers were printed up to announce the boycott. An army of volunteers distributed them in the city's black neighborhoods. Black ministers talked about the protest in their Sunday sermons and urged everyone in their congregations to support it.

Volunteers posted hand-lettered signs urging blacks to support the bus boycott. This one read: "Reme[m]ber We Are Fighting For a Cause. Do Not Ride A Bus Today."

The boycott was a bold idea, and no one knew if it would work. Blacks might be afraid to stay off the buses for fear of being attacked by members of the Ku Klux Klan— a secret society of **white supremacists** who intimidated and terrorized blacks.

There was also the question of how the city's forty thousand black bus riders would get around the city. Few of them owned cars. Buses were their only means of transportation. The city's black-owned taxi companies stepped in and ordered their drivers to pick up

A Montgomery bus during the boycott. The signs separating the white and the negro sections have been removed, but there are still no passengers. Organizers refused to call off the boycott until all their demands were met.

blacks at the bus stops and take them wherever they needed to go. The charge would be the same as the bus fare—ten cents.

On Monday morning, Coretta Scott King looked out her front window. A bus on the South Jackson line, which ran past the parsonage, was driving by without a single passenger. "Martin, Martin, come quickly," Coretta called.

King rushed to the window in time to see the empty bus. A few minutes later, another bus appeared, then another and another and another. All of them were empty.

King drove over to the First Baptist Church and picked up Ralph Abernathy. They rode around the city, checking out the other bus lines. None of them had any black passengers. The boycott was a success.

Ralph Abernathy (1926–1990)

One of the first people Martin Luther King, Jr., met when he moved to Montgomery was Ralph Abernathy, pastor of the city's First Baptist Church. Abernathy was almost three years older than King. He had grown up poor in rural Alabama and lacked King's social polish. He was also less scholarly than King.

In spite of their differences, the two men became friends. They shared a sense of humor and liked to entertain their wives with imitations of some of the more pompous ministers in town. When the Montgomery bus boycott began, they discovered that they also shared a desire to secure equal treatment for African Americans.

Martin Luther King, Jr., once described his close friend the Reverend Ralph David Abernathy as a persuasive and dynamic speaker who had "the gift of laughing people into positive action."

The two ministers became almost inseparable. Abernathy was at Martin Luther King, Jr.'s side all during the civil rights movement and was jailed with him more than a dozen times. Many people believe that their friendship bolstered King's self-esteem and contributed to his success as a leader.

Hundreds of African Americans walked to their jobs during the 381-day bus boycott. In discussing the protest, Martin Luther King, Jr., often mentioned the elderly woman who told him, "My feets is tired, but my soul is rested."

The Montgomery Improvement Association

On the afternoon of December 5, the black leaders held another meeting. They agreed to continue the boycott and form an organization—the Montgomery Improvement Association (MIA)—to manage it. King was elected president. The black leaders could not agree on how long the boycott should last, so they decided to take a vote at the public meeting that would be held that evening at the Holt Street Baptist Church.

As president of the MIA, King would deliver the main speech at the meeting. He did not have time to labor over every sentence as he did with his Sunday sermons. All he could do was jot down a few notes.

The point he wanted to emphasize was that the protest— however long it lasted—would be peaceful. "We are not here advocating violence," he said. "We have overcome that. I want it to be known throughout Montgomery and throughout this nation

Carpools provided transportation for many blacks during the boycott. In addition, several of the city's black churches purchased station wagons and painted their names on the sides. The vehicles became known as rolling churches.

that we are Christian people. . . . The only weapon that we have in our hands this evening is the weapon of protest."

Ralph Abernathy was next on the program. He announced that he and King had drawn up a list of demands that the bus company would have to meet if they expected to end the boycott. The list included hiring black drivers and ordering white drivers to stop insulting black passengers. It also stipulated that blacks occupying seats in the black section of the bus did not have to give them up if whites got on at later stops.

When Abernathy finished reading the list of demands, he called for a vote. He asked all those who wanted to continue the boycott until the bus company met the demands to stand. Everyone in the church stood up.

The Boycott

During the early weeks of the bus boycott, Montgomery's city commissioners tried to end it. They were embarrassed by the negative press coverage the boycott was getting and alarmed by the fact that, without its black riders, the bus company was sliding into bankruptcy. The commissioners threatened to fine any taxi driver who charged less than the standard fare, but King outwitted them by organizing a gigantic carpool. The MIA found black car owners to serve as volunteer drivers and raised money—much of it from sympathetic whites—to buy a fleet of station wagons to carry the overflow.

King's home was flooded with hate mail. One night, he received a chilling phone call. "Listen, nigger," said a voice at the other end of the line, "we've taken all we want from you. Before next week you'll be sorry you ever came to Montgomery."

A few nights later, King was speaking at an MIA meeting when he received word that his house had been bombed. He rushed home and discovered that the blast had destroyed the porch and shattered the front windows. Thankfully, Coretta and baby Yolanda were unhurt. They had been in another part of the house when the bomb went off.

After King's home was bombed in February 1956, the minister stood on his damaged front porch with a group of Montgomery city officials and assured a crowd of angry blacks that he and his family were safe.

King's next concern was the crowd of angry blacks who had gathered on the street outside. They were armed with broken bottles. A few of them carried guns. The white police officers at the scene were having trouble keeping order. King stepped out on his battered front porch and held up his hand. The crowd fell silent. He assured them that his family was safe and his house could be repaired. He told them to put down their weapons. There was no need for violence. "We must meet hate with love," he said.

The crowd slowly dispersed, and the police officers breathed a sigh of relief. The Kings spent the night at the home of friends.

FOR Lends a Hand

The Montgomery bus boycott was widely reported in the media. The news stories captured the attention of a black activist from New York named Bayard Rustin, who went to Montgomery to get a firsthand look at the protest.

Rustin belonged to the Fellowship of Reconciliation (FOR), an organization that had been founded in England shortly before World War I with the goal of promoting world peace through nonviolent means. Like all FOR members, Rustin was a disciple of Mahatma Gandhi. He saw at once that Martin Luther King, Jr., was preaching the same message of

A member of the Fellowship of Reconciliation (FOR), Bayard Rustin, helped King obtain nonviolent training for the Montgomery boycotters. Rustin spent most of his life working for social and political causes.

nonviolence that Gandhi had preached and using the same weapon: **civil disobedience**. He also saw that although King had the Gandhian spirit, he did not have Gandhi's experience in dealing with the consequences of demonstrating against established laws.

Rustin contacted FOR headquarters in New York and warned them that the bus boycott would collapse unless the boycotters got some training in Gandhi's tactics. FOR's national field secretary, a white minister named Glen Smiley, hurried to Montgomery to provide it.

During the next few months, Smiley made many visits to the city. He instructed the boycotters on the methods Gandhi had used to help his followers withstand the abuses the British authorities inflicted on them. He taught the boycotters how to remain calm when they were insulted and spat upon, how to avoid serious injuries when they were attacked with clubs and nightsticks, and how to survive in filthy, foul-smelling jail cells.

"We must meet hate with love," he said.

Smiley's instructions were helpful, but in Montgomery the main problem was police harassment. Carpool drivers were stopped and questioned for no reason or given tickets for minor or nonexistent traffic violations. One afternoon, King was put in jail for driving thirty miles an hour in a twenty-five-mile zone.

Glen Smiley nevertheless made a welcome contribution to the Montgomery bus boycott. His guidance and moral support strengthened King's commitment to nonviolence and gave him a deeper understanding of Gandhi's work.

A Federal Lawsuit

One of the two black attorneys in Montgomery, Fred Gray, also served as legal counsel to the local chapter of the NAACP. Gray urged the MIA to let him file a federal lawsuit against segregated buses. If he won, the practice would become illegal not only in Montgomery, but everywhere else in the country.

King and the other MIA leaders agreed that a federal lawsuit offered the best hope of success. Although Rosa Parks had appealed her conviction, her case was being tried in the state courts, where racist judges were unlikely to give her a fair hearing. On February 1, Gray filed a lawsuit in a U.S. district court on behalf of four other black women, all of them longtime opponents of segregated buses. The suit charged that the bus company had discriminated against the women by not allowing them to sit wherever they pleased. It would be months before the suit was settled. The MIA leaders agreed that the boycott would continue until it was.

Victory

In another attempt to end the **stalemate**, Montgomery's city commissioners dredged up an old and rarely invoked law against boycotts. They used it to arrest King and more than eighty other black leaders on charges of instigating a boycott. The mass arrests brought reporters flocking to Montgomery. As president of the MIA, King was considered the instigator of the boycott and thus

Martin Luther King, Jr., leaves the Montgomery courthouse with Coretta after he was found guilty of instigating a boycott. The arrests of the boycott leaders created sympathy for the protestors and resulted in more than $200,000 in donations to the Montgomery Improvement Association (MIA).

was the first to be tried. The trial gave the press their first look at the youthful civil rights leader. They came away impressed. King was convicted and fined $500, plus another $500 in court costs. The charges against the other black leaders were dismissed.

As the boycott dragged on, the city commissioners came up with another idea. They applied for a court order to ban the MIA car pool as an unlicensed transportation system. The order was granted, but before it could be enforced the four black women whom Fred Gray represented won their suit against the bus company. Their case had gone all the way to the Supreme Court, where the justices upheld the district court ruling. Segregated buses, like segregated schools, were unconstitutional.

The written order was delivered to the city commissioners on December 20, 1956—381 days after the boycott began. Early the next morning, Martin Luther King, Jr., Ralph Abernathy, Fred Gray, and Glen Smiley rode through Montgomery on the city's first integrated bus.

U.S. District Courts

U.S. district courts are the courts in which cases involving federal laws are heard. There are ninety-four federal judicial districts in the United States with at least one district in each state and others in the District of Columbia and Puerto Rico.

The federal judicial districts are organized into regional circuits, each of which has a U.S. court of appeals. When a lawyer loses a case in district court, he can try to get the decision reversed by taking the case to the court of appeals. If the case involves important questions about federal law or interpretations of the Constitution, the U.S. Supreme Court may review it and issue a final decision.

Following the Supreme Court ruling that segregated buses were unconstitutional, Ralph Abernathy (front row, right), Glen Smiley (second row, left), and Martin Luther King, Jr., (second row, right) are shown riding on an integrated bus in Montgomery.

Although the Supreme Court ruling was the decisive factor in bringing the boycott to a successful conclusion, the impact of the boycott cannot be underestimated. Instead of waiting for the nation's leaders to solve their problems as they had been doing since the Civil War, African Americans had taken matters into their own hands. By doing so, they had not only achieved a major victory, they had found a way to make white people aware of their plight.

CHAPTER 5

The Southern Christian Leadership Conference

History has thrust upon me a responsibility from which I cannot turn away.

Within days of the victory in Montgomery, bus boycotts were organized in three other Southern cities— Birmingham and Mobile in Alabama, and Tallahassee in Florida. King was glad to see the protests spreading, but he thought their leaders should be working together as part of a larger protest against segregation. He and Ralph Abernathy, along with two other ministers, Charles K. Steele of Tallahassee and Fred Shuttlesworth of Birmingham, called a meeting of black clergymen from ten Southern states to discuss the formation of a permanent civil rights organization.

Students at all-black Florida A&M College wave at the driver of an empty city bus. The photograph was taken during the 1956 boycott of segregated bus lines in Tallahassee, Florida.

The meeting was held in Atlanta on January 10 and 11, 1957. King and Abernathy had barely arrived in the city when Abernathy's wife called to tell him that his church and their home had been bombed. A number of other black churches and parsonages had suffered the same fate. Montgomery had been struck by a wave of violence when the Supreme Court ruling against segregated buses went into effect. Gun-toting whites were shooting at buses to express their outrage at **integration**, and Ku Klux Klansmen were burning crosses—the Klan's trademark act—to frighten blacks into ignoring the decision.

After hearing that news, King and Abernathy flew back to Montgomery. King returned to Atlanta the next day, but by then the meeting was almost over. Both men attended a second meeting in New Orleans, where some sixty black ministers formed the Southern Christian Leadership Conference (SCLC). King was elected president, and Abernathy, treasurer.

One of the SCLC's first moves was to contact President Dwight D. Eisenhower and ask him to enforce both *Brown v. Board of Education of Topeka* and the Supreme Court ruling against segregation on buses. The two decisions were being almost totally ignored. When the president did not respond, the SCLC contacted him again. This time they asked him to call a White House conference on civil rights. Again there was no response.

The Prayer Pilgrimage for Freedom

When the SCLC was rebuffed by the White House, two longtime black activists took matters into their own hands. Labor leader A. Philip Randolph and Roy Wilkins, executive secretary of the NAACP, invited King to join them in leading a "Prayer Pilgrimage for Freedom."

The SCLC Name

During the thirteen months that the Montgomery bus boycott was in effect, Martin Luther King, Jr., and Ralph Abernathy traveled around the South, meeting with other black ministers and urging them to support the boycott. When King and Abernathy decided to form a permanent civil rights organization, they turned to the clergy for help. Ministers had a great deal of authority in the black community and would have no trouble persuading their congregations to join the movement. In addition, their churches could be used as centers for meetings and rallies.

King was constantly on the road making speeches to raise funds for the Southern Christian Leadership Conference (SCLC). In the beginning, his audiences were largely black. He is shown here greeting parishioners at a Baptist church in Miami.

The ministers who founded the new organization realized that it needed a name that would disguise its true purpose. The one they selected was the Southern Christian Leadership Conference. The word "Christian" in the title would make Southern whites think it was simply an association of Baptist preachers, a group not usually known for causing trouble.

Seated on the speakers' platform at the 1957 Prayer Pilgrimage for Freedom are (left to right) Roy Wilkins, A. Philip Randolph, the Reverend Thomas Kilgore, Jr., and Martin Luther King, Jr. Kilgore was the director of the pilgrimage.

The pilgrimage was to be held in Washington, D.C., on May 17, 1957. The date would mark the third anniversary of *Brown v. Board of Education of Topeka.* Randolph and Wilkins wanted to remind the country that, despite the decision, most of the South's public schools were still segregated.

On May 17, some twenty thousand people gathered in front of the Lincoln Memorial. They heard music by black entertainers and speeches by black activists, but the star of the Prayer Pilgrimage was Martin Luther King, Jr. King's speech was a plea to the federal government to enforce the Fifteenth Amendment to the Constitution.

Although the amendment gave blacks the right to vote, those who lived in the South were rarely allowed to cast their ballots. In his speech, King noted that "all types of conniving methods are still being used to prevent Negroes from becoming registered voters. The denial of this sacred right is a tragic betrayal of the highest mandates of our democratic tradition. And so our most urgent request to

Although the amendment gave blacks the right to vote, those who lived in the South were rarely allowed to cast their ballots.

the president of the United States and every member of Congress is to give us the right to vote."

The Montgomery bus boycott had made Martin Luther King, Jr., a national figure. His speech at the Prayer Pilgrimage made him even more famous. One African American newspaper called him "the number one leader of sixteen million Negroes in the United States." Vice President Richard M. Nixon met with King, and one of President Eisenhower's cabinet members called to express the president's interest in meeting him. Although nothing came of either of the conversations, they marked the first time anyone in the Eisenhower White House had reached out to a black leader.

A Brush with Death

During the bus boycott, King had toured the country making speeches to raise money for the protest. Now he began doing the same thing for the SCLC. Between his travels and his pastoral duties, he had little time for family life. When Coretta gave birth to their second child, Martin III, he was conducting a business meeting at his church. To the disapproval of the churchwomen, he waited until the meeting was over before going to the hospital.

Coretta knew that her husband loved his family, but she also knew that his responsibilities to his church and to the civil rights movement would always come first. She and their children were often left alone while Martin was busy elsewhere. Having a part-time husband and father was their contribution to the cause.

In the midst of his hectic schedule, King found time to write his first book, *Stride Toward Freedom: The Montgomery Story*. Stanley Levison, a wealthy New Yorker whom he had met on one of his speaking tours, edited it and found him a publisher. Levison was among the first white supporters of the civil rights

The Little Rock Nine

Southern school systems were slow to comply with *Brown v. Board of Education of Topeka*. The city of Little Rock, Arkansas, was among the worst. It did not begin to integrate its schools until three years after the decision. The process would have been delayed even longer if the U.S. district court had not stepped in and ordered the city to obey the law.

On September 3, 1957, nine black students, who soon became known as the Little Rock Nine, showed up for classes at Little Rock's Central High School. They found members of the Arkansas National Guard blocking the door. Governor Orval Faubus had called out the troops and instructed them to keep the blacks from entering the school.

On September 20, a U.S. district court judge ordered Faubus to remove the troops. The Little Rock Nine could now enter the school, but to do so they had to pass a mob of whites shouting racial slurs and pelting them with bricks. When the Little Rock police were unable to control the mob, President Dwight D. Eisenhower sent the U.S. Army's 101st Airborne Division to the scene with orders to enforce the law. The Little Rock Nine finished the school year under the protection of federal troops.

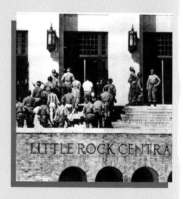

"The Little Rock Nine" are shown entering Central High School in 1958 under the watchful eyes of federal troops. The school is now a National Historic Site and has a museum and visitors' center run by the National Park Service.

movement. The book appeared in the fall of 1958 and became a how-to manual for other civil rights groups.

When *Stride Toward Freedom* was published, Martin Luther King went on a tour to promote it. During a book signing at a department store in New York City's Harlem, a well-dressed black woman approached him and asked if he was Martin Luther King, Jr. When he told her he was, she said, "I've been looking for you for five years." With that, she stabbed him in the chest with a steel letter opener.

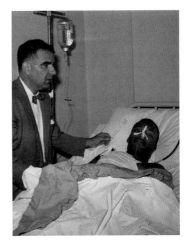

A doctor at Harlem Hospital examines King after a steel letter opener was removed from his chest. King told the horrified crowd who witnessed the assault, "Everything is going to be all right."

King was rushed to Harlem Hospital, where surgeons spent three hours removing the weapon from his chest. It was lodged next to his aorta, the main artery from his heart. If it had been a fraction of an inch closer, it would have ruptured the artery and killed him. King's attacker, a seriously disturbed woman named Izola Curry, was committed to a hospital for the criminally insane.

Farewell to Dexter

King's nonviolent protest in Montgomery brought him to the attention of Gandhi's admirers in the United States. One of them insisted that he visit India to learn more about Gandhi's career. The man arranged for a foundation to pay his way, and in February of 1959 Martin and Coretta took a monthlong trip to

India. They had dinner with Prime Minister Jawaharlal Nehru, met with one of Gandhi's chief lieutenants, and laid a wreath on the Indian leader's tomb.

The trip was a memorable experience, but when King returned to Atlanta he was upset to discover that the SCLC was on the verge of bankruptcy. He had to embark on a speaking tour to raise enough money to keep it afloat. King had never planned to be a hands-on leader of the SCLC. He had expected to raise funds and rally support for its projects and let a staff member manage its day-to-day operations. The problems that had arisen in his absence made him realize that he would have to be more directly involved.

When King visited India, he met with Jawaharlal Nehru, India's first prime minister. Nehru had worked with Mahatma Gandhi in the struggle to win independence for India.

On November 29, 1959, King announced his resignation as pastor of Dexter Avenue Baptist Church. He apologized to his congregation for neglecting them during the previous four years. As president of the MIA, he had become absorbed in the civil rights movement. Now he was too involved to give it up. In his farewell sermon, he said, "History has thrust upon me a responsibility from which I cannot turn away."

Early in 1960, Martin and Coretta King and their two children moved to Atlanta. They settled into a redbrick house near Ebenezer Baptist Church. King was to be his father's co-pastor, but his main job would be leading the SCLC.

CHAPTER 6

Political Power

Mr. Kennedy has done some significant things in civil rights, but I do not feel that he has yet given the leadership that the enormity of the problem demands.

In the 1960 presidential election, Daddy King and the other black leaders in Atlanta were supporting the Republican candidate, Richard M. Nixon. Blacks had been loyal to the party of Abraham Lincoln ever since they got the vote. Although Martin Luther King, Jr., was leaning toward Nixon's Democratic opponent, John F. Kennedy, he decided to remain neutral. He was angry at both parties for refusing to take a stand on civil rights. Although President Eisenhower had sent federal troops to integrate the schools in Little Rock, Arkansas, he did so to uphold the law, not to advance the cause of civil rights.

A Shift in Black Votes

In an effort to boost Kennedy's popularity among blacks, a Democratic campaign aide asked King to meet with the candidate. King agreed, but to maintain his neutrality he told the aide that he planned to seek a meeting with Nixon as well. Kennedy knew that a meeting with the Republican candidate would further enhance Nixon's standing among black voters. Unwilling to see that happen, Kennedy cancelled their meeting.

A 1960 campaign poster for Democrat John F. Kennedy. During the 1960 presidential election, both Kennedy and his Republican opponent, Richard M. Nixon, tried to win the black vote.

King's meeting with Kennedy had been scheduled for the same day that the Atlanta chapter of the Student Nonviolent Coordinating Committee (SNCC, pronounced "snick") planned to stage **sit-ins** at the restaurants of Atlanta's largest department stores, where blacks were not allowed to eat. The SNCC leaders had been begging King to join them. They expected to go to jail, and they wanted King to go with them. His presence would get maximum attention for their protest.

The meeting with Kennedy had given King a good excuse to turn the students down. Although his heart was with them, he thought SNCC should conduct its own protests. He also knew that his arrest would embarrass his father, who disapproved of sit-ins. Like most older African Americans, Daddy King thought blacks should fight for their rights in the courts, not in the streets.

The day before the sit-in, the head of the Atlanta chapter of SNCC called King with one last plea to join the protest. With no excuse to say no, King cast aside his doubts and promised to meet the students at Rich's department store at ten o'clock the next morning.

On the morning of October 19, King and the students tried to enter the restaurant at Rich's. They were turned away at the door. When they refused to leave, they were arrested for trespassing. The judge who heard their case gave them a choice of posting **bail** or being sent to jail. They chose jail.

Atlanta's mayor, William Hartsfield, was appalled to learn that the country's most prominent Negro was a prisoner in his city's jail. Hartsfield was one of the rare Southern politicians who was working to improve race relations. He did not want anything to interfere with his efforts.

The mayor managed to get the charges against the students dropped, but King's case was more difficult. Some months earlier, the civil rights leader had been arrested for a minor traffic violation. Because this was his second offense, he was denied bail and sentenced to four months at hard labor in the state penitentiary. Coretta King, who was pregnant with their third

Coretta Scott King gives her husband a welcome-home kiss after he was released from Reidsville State Prison. Joining the crowd of well-wishers are the Kings' children, Yolanda, five, and Martin Luther King III, three.

The Student Nonviolent Coordinating Committee

The success of the Montgomery boycott inspired other nonviolent direct-action campaigns. Early in 1960, four students at the all-black North Carolina Agricultural and Technical College in Greensboro staged a sit-in at the white-only lunch counter of a downtown department store. When a waitress refused to take their order, the students remained in their seats until the store closed. Soon after that, another group of students from Fisk University in Nashville, Tennessee, staged a sit-in at six of Nashville's white-only lunch counters. The protests became so popular that by the summer of 1961, over seventy thousand students had participated in sit-ins in dozens of Southern cities.

In 1960, college students Joseph McNeil, Franklin McCain, Billy Smith, and Clarence Henderson staged the civil rights movement's first sit-in at a lunch counter in Greensboro, North Carolina. Later, white college students in the North conducted sit-ins to show their sympathy for the blacks.

Martin Luther King, Jr., wanted the student activists to become part of the SCLC, but the young people preferred to form their own civil rights organization. They signaled their agreement with King's policy of peaceful protests, however, by calling it the Student Nonviolent Coordinating Committee, or SNCC.

child (Dexter, who was born in January of 1961), collapsed in tears when she heard the verdict.

Hartsfield called John F. Kennedy's campaign headquarters to see if the candidate could or would get King's sentence reversed. Kennedy refused. If word got out that he had helped King, he would lose millions of white votes in the South.

One of Kennedy's advisers suggested that he might at least call Coretta and express his sympathies on her husband's imprisonment. Kennedy made the call, but his brother Robert went a step further. He contacted the judge in the case and reminded him that it was illegal to deny bail for a misdemeanor. The judge revised his decision, and a few days later King was released on bail.

Somehow, the story of Kennedy's call to Coretta Scott King got into the newspapers. That year, more African Americans voted for a Democratic president than ever before. Daddy King was among them. Although Kennedy probably lost the votes of many white Southerners, as he had feared, it is generally agreed that a shift in black votes in several Northern states was the key to his victory.

Dangerous Journeys

Four months after John F. Kennedy took office, a racially mixed group of young people, who called themselves Freedom Riders, was viciously beaten by white mobs in Anniston and Birmingham, Alabama. The young people had been traveling on buses throughout the South deliberately disobeying the drivers' orders to sit in separate sections and use separate

. . . A racially-mixed group of young people, who called themselves Freedom Riders, was viciously beaten by white mobs in Anniston and Birmingham, Alabama.

Changing Sides

After the Civil War, Southerners, angry at the Republicans for starting the war, became ardent Democrats. They regarded the former slaves as second-class citizens and enacted Jim Crow laws to keep them "in their place"—separate and submissive to whites. The Democratic Party dominated Southern politics for almost a century. They also wielded immense amounts of power in national elections, sending Democratic senators and representatives to Congress and providing a solid block of votes for Democratic presidential candidates.

The civil rights movement caused a major shift in party loyalties. Northern Democrats broke with Southerners over the issue, and the Southerners began moving into the ranks of the Republicans. Meanwhile, African Americans, who had traditionally been Republicans, were moving in the opposite direction. In recent years, blacks throughout the country have consistently voted for Democratic candidates while the majority of Southern whites cast their ballots for Republicans.

facilities in the terminals. The Freedom Riders were protesting the fact that the Supreme Court rulings against segregation in interstate travel were not being enforced.

The beatings presented Kennedy with a **dilemma**. He knew the law was on the side of the Freedom Riders, but he did not want to lose the support of white Southerners. The surprising number of votes from Northern blacks had made the difference in an exceedingly close election, but Kennedy had also won substantial majorities in such segregationist strongholds as Arkansas, Georgia, Louisiana, and the Carolinas.

Kennedy's brother Robert—now the attorney general—sent one of his aides, John Seigenthaler, to Alabama as the president's personal representative. Kennedy hoped that the presence of a federal official would discourage any further violence. The attorney general also asked Alabama Governor John Patterson to guarantee the Freedom Riders' safety. Patterson would not commit himself. He told Kennedy that the state of Alabama would do its best to protect the Freedom Riders but he could not be responsible for the actions of its outraged citizens.

A week later, a new group of Freedom Riders arrived in Birmingham to complete the journey that had been interrupted by the attacks. They boarded a bus to Montgomery, the next stop on the trip to Mississippi. When they reached the Montgomery bus terminal, they were met by a swarm of Ku Klux Klansmen armed with baseball bats and pipes. Several of the Freedom Riders were seriously hurt. John Seigenthaler, who arrived at the terminal in the middle of the conflict, was knocked unconscious.

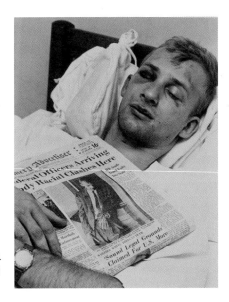

In May 1961, white Freedom Rider Jim Zwerg was severely beaten by segregationists in Montgomery. One man seized the 21-year-old's suitcase and smashed him in the face with it. Others punched him until most of his teeth were knocked out.

The Freedom Riders

In 1946, the U.S. Supreme Court declared that segregated seating on interstate buses and trains was unconstitutional. In many parts of the South, the decision was ignored. In 1960, the court issued a second decision against segregated bus and train terminals. A year later, civil rights activist James Farmer, one of the founders of the Congress of Racial Equality (CORE), decided to find out if the second ruling was also being ignored.

A group calling themselves the Washington Freedom Riders Committee prepares to leave New York City on May 30, 1961. The young people hoped to meet with officials of the Kennedy administration to demand federal action on civil rights.

Farmer recruited a group of young people, both blacks and whites, to become Freedom Riders. The whites would sit in the back of the bus and the blacks in front. When they were asked to move, both groups would refuse. When they got to a bus terminal, they would follow the same routine. The blacks would use the white-only waiting rooms, and the whites would use the ones for "coloreds."

"This was not civil disobedience, really, because we were merely doing what the Supreme Court said we have a right to do," Farmer said later. "We felt we could count on the racists of the South to create a crisis so that the federal government would be compelled to enforce the law."

Menaced by a Mob

On Sunday, May 21, King flew into Montgomery to speak at a rally in support of the Freedom Riders. By eight o'clock that evening, some fifteen hundred people had gathered in Ralph Abernathy's First Baptist Church. An even larger crowd of inflamed whites had assembled in a park across the street. Not long after the rally started, the noisy and menacing crowd began moving toward the church.

The minister who was presiding at the rally tried to distract the audience by leading them in hymns. The audience sang as loudly as they could but they were unable to drown out the noise from the street. Bottles filled with gasoline were hurled at the church. A brick hit a stained-glass window, showering many of the people inside with broken glass.

After the attack in Birmingham, Attorney General Robert Kennedy had dispatched six hundred **federal marshals** to Alabama. Governor Patterson assured him they would not be needed. Kennedy took the governor at his word and ordered the marshals to be used sparingly.

U.S. marshals, wearing armbands, attempt to hold back the mob of segregationists who were trying to storm the First Baptist Church in Montgomery.

U.S. marshals used tear gas to drive back the mob at the First Baptist Church. When the gas seeped into the church, some of the rally-goers rushed outside in search of fresh air.

A dozen marshals stood guard at the First Baptist Church, hardly enough to control such a large crowd. They called for reinforcements, and a second detachment of marshals arrived. They fired off tear gas, which drove away some of the rioters. Unfortunately, it also drifted into the church and left the people inside gasping for breath. While the ushers rushed to close the windows, the frightened blacks could hear pounding at the back door of the church. The mob was trying to break it down.

Fearful of what might happen next, King retreated to a church office and called Attorney General Kennedy. He told him that the people in the First Baptist Church needed federal protection as soon as possible. They were in danger of being killed. Not long after that, the noise outside abated. The blacks assumed that the attorney general had responded to King's call by asking President Kennedy to send the U.S. Army to protect them. Reassured, they settled down to hear Martin Luther King, Jr.

"The main thing I want to say to you tonight is fear not, we've come too far to turn back," King told his listeners. "We are not afraid and we shall overcome."

It was nearly midnight when King finished speaking. The weary rally-goers headed for the door only to discover that the troops outside were members of the Alabama National Guard. They had been sent not by President Kennedy but by Governor Patterson. Their commanding officer had dismissed the federal marshals and ordered his men to prevent the blacks

"We are not afraid and we shall overcome."

from leaving the church. The officer told them that the mob was still outside, and he did not want the blacks to be attacked.

King was desperate to get his people out of the building. They had not eaten or slept for hours. Many of them had family members at home who would be worried about their safety. Angry at both Kennedys for not sending the federal troops he had asked for, King put in another call to the attorney general. He demanded to know if there was law and order in the United States.

An infuriated Robert Kennedy got on the phone to Governor Patterson. After a heated argument, Patterson ordered the Alabama National Guard to disperse the mob and escort King and his followers out of the church. By the time they left, it was 4:30 a.m.

CHAPTER 7

The Albany Movement

This is one time I'm out of jail that I'm not happy to be out.

In December 1961, Martin Luther King, Jr., received an urgent request from Dr. William Anderson, the president of the Albany Movement, a group of civil rights activists in Albany, Georgia. The movement, which had been organized that fall, was trying to desegregate the city's schools, parks, and other public places and increase the number of African American voters. So far, they had had no success.

Every time the movement held a demonstration, Albany's police chief, Laurie Pritchett, arrested the demonstrators. By the time Anderson contacted King, more than five hundred protestors were in jail. Chief Pritchett had done some homework on nonviolent protests. He knew that one of the ways Gandhi had forced the British to negotiate with him was by turning out so many demonstrators that the jails could not hold them all. Pritchett did not intend to let that happen in Albany.

The city's jail had room for only thirty prisoners. Pritchett coped with the cell shortage by getting in touch with the police chiefs in every town within thirty miles of Albany and arranging to have the protestors put in their jails.

Pritchett also made a point of arresting the protestors for violating **municipal** laws, such as loitering, disturbing

Pray-ins were a favorite form of protest in Albany, Georgia. After warning these demonstrators that they were violating a city ordinance against parading without a permit, Police Chief Laurie Pritchett had them arrested.

the peace, or parading without a permit. This prevented them from being tried in the U.S. district court, which only heard cases involving federal laws. If the protestors' cases had gone to the federal court, Albany's segregation laws would have been overturned.

A Call for King's Help

William Anderson wanted King to appear at one of the Albany Movement's rallies. A pep talk from King would energize the discouraged protestors and might induce Chief Pritchett and Albany's mayor, Asa Kelley, to negotiate with them.

The rally was held on Friday evening, December 15, at the Shiloh Baptist Church. King, who arrived with Ralph Abernathy, had to fight his way into the church. An enormous crowd stood outside, chanting, "FREE-DOM, FREE-DOM."

King spoke in his usual eloquent style. He encouraged the protestors to persevere, but reminded them of the hardships that lay ahead. "Before the victory is won," he said, "some must face physical death to free their children from a life of psychological handicaps. But we shall overcome."

"Shall overcome," came the echoing roar from his listeners.

King had planned to return to Atlanta that night, but Anderson called for a march on City Hall the next morning. Carried away by the enthusiasm of the crowd, King agreed to lead it.

On Saturday morning, Chief Pritchett arrested 250 demonstrators, including King and Abernathy, for parading without a permit. King refused to post bail, vowing to remain in jail until Albany was integrated. Abernathy bailed himself out because he had to conduct services at his church the next day.

Two days later, King was informed that Mayor Kelley and Chief Pritchett had agreed to release the demonstrators and negotiate with the leaders of the Albany Movement—but only if

King leads a line of protestors down the main street of Albany, Georgia. Unfortunately, the demonstration was unsuccessful, and King told his associates that he would not participate in any more protests unless he planned and led them himself.

We Shall Overcome

"We shall overcome" was the favorite rallying cry of King's followers. The words were taken from the song "We Shall Overcome," became the theme song of the civil rights movement.

The song was originally a religious folk tune. In 1901, C. Albert Tindley, a Baptist minister in Philadelphia, turned it into a hymn, "I'll Overcome Some Day." During a 1946 strike by African American women at a tobacco company plant in Charleston, South Carolina, the first words were changed to "we shall" and the women sang the song on the picket line.

The phrase "We shall overcome" became the rallying cry for the civil rights movement. In a San Francisco civil rights march in 1963, a participant is seen holding a sign with the inspiring words.

Some years later, members of the labor movement taught the song to folksinger Pete Seeger. In 1960, Seeger and two other folksingers, Frank Hamilton and Guy Carawan, rewrote the lyrics and composed a new musical arrangement. Carawan, who was in Nashville, Tennessee, during the lunch counter sit-ins, popularized the song among the student demonstrators. Two of them introduced the now-famous version to the Albany Movement.

King left town. King was bailed out by a group of local residents and left Albany, explaining that he "did not want to stand in the way of peaceful negotiations." When he got home to Atlanta, however, the SCLC leader discovered that the officials had no intention of negotiating. The story had been invented to get him out of Albany.

Choosing Jail Time

In February, King and Abernathy returned to Albany to stand trial for parading without a permit. Although the judge promised to deliver his verdict within sixty days, it took him until July to do it. He found the two men guilty and gave them a choice of paying a $178 fine or spending forty-five days in jail. They both chose jail. Paying the fine would have gained little attention for the civil rights movement, but the jailing of America's most famous black leader would—and did—make headlines around the world.

Paying the fine would have gained little attention . . . but the jailing of America's most famous black leader would—and did—make headlines around the world.

When President John F. Kennedy heard about King's sentence, he asked Attorney General Robert Kennedy to look into the matter. The president realized that King's jailing was a national disgrace, but he was reluctant to get involved in the dispute. If he arranged for King's release, he would antagonize the Southern Democrats in Congress. As president, he needed their votes to get his programs enacted. Kennedy was hoping that Albany's mayor would negotiate a settlement and not force him to intervene.

After investigating the situation in Albany, Attorney General Kennedy reported that no federal laws were being violated. The dispute was a purely local matter. Both the attorney general and the president were concerned, however, that King's jailing was damaging America's reputation abroad. It was hard to claim that the United States guaranteed equal rights to all its citizens when Albany, Georgia, offered stark proof that it did not.

The jailing was also damaging Albany's reputation. Mayor Kelley wanted to see King released but he did not want to appear to be giving in to the blacks. James Gray, the editor of Albany's newspaper and a former New Englander who was a personal friend of John F. Kennedy's, called the president to see what could be done. Kennedy advised Gray to send someone to Washington to confer with the attorney general.

Three days later, King and Abernathy were abruptly released. According to Chief Pritchett, a "well-dressed Negro male" had paid their fine. A few years later it was revealed that Pritchett had been lying. The "well-dressed Negro male" had been one of Mayor Asa Kelley's law partners, a white man; he was acting on confidential advice from the attorney general, who, along with Kelley, was eager to get King and Abernathy out of the spotlight.

Ralph Abernathy, Martin Luther King, Jr., and Dr. William Anderson (far right) after being released from jail in Albany, Georgia, in July 1962. In the eight months he worked with the Albany Movement, King was jailed three times.

The ex-prisoners were angry at being released. They knew that as long as they were in jail, the Albany Movement would be in the news, and the negative publicity might embarrass Mayor Kelley into making **concessions**.

"This is one time I'm out of jail that I'm not happy to be out," King told reporters.

A Hopeless Situation

Unwilling to give up, King returned to Albany with a team of SCLC staff members. When Mayor Kelley refused to meet with him, he pledged to "fill up the jails" and "turn Albany upside down."

On July 20, while King and Anderson were making plans for another march, they were served with a temporary **injunction** issued by a federal district judge. It called for the civil rights demonstrations to stop until the judge could hold a hearing on the city's request for a permanent injunction.

Four days later, an appeals court judge set the injunction aside, allowing the demonstrations to resume. The next day, two thousand blacks staged a protest after white jail guards beat up a black woman who had been taking food to some of the jailed protestors. Disregarding King's rules against violence, the protestors began throwing rocks and bottles at the police. King called for a "Day of Penance" to atone for their rowdy behavior.

Some of the younger demonstrators thought King's anger should have been directed at the white jail guards rather than the protestors. They laughed at him behind his back and made fun of his talk about Christian principles. King was also becoming unpopular among the older members of the Albany

King was also becoming unpopular among the older members of the Albany Movement.

Movement. Many of them resented the SCLC's involvement in the protest. They thought King was trying to upstage them and make himself the center of attention.

King made one final effort to keep the Albany Movement from collapsing. He and Abernathy held a prayer meeting in front of City Hall. They were arrested for causing a public disturbance and remained in jail for two weeks. When their case came to trial, the judge found them guilty. He sentenced each of them to a $200 fine and sixty days in jail, then abruptly suspended the sentences and told them they were free to go. The judge knew that another jail sentence would only have given them more attention.

Embarrassed and discouraged, King was forced to acknowledge that the situation in Albany was hopeless. After almost a year and a half of protests, the city was as segregated as it had ever been.

Demonstrators praying in front of City Hall in Albany, Georgia. After King left Albany, seventy-five Northerners, including ministers and rabbis, arrived to join the protest. They, too, were taken to jail.

CHAPTER 8

Birmingham

We have waited for more than 340 years for our constitutional and God-given rights.

After his failure in Albany, Martin Luther King, Jr., was determined to stage a successful civil rights demonstration. Equally important, he wanted to get President John F. Kennedy's attention. Kennedy had sent a civil rights bill to Congress not long after he took office, but he had made no effort to get it passed and the bill was soon forgotten. King wanted the president to send another bill to Congress and to put the full power of his presidency behind it. A federal law was the only way African Americans could be fully assured of gaining their civil rights.

Early in 1962, King met with his staff at the SCLC to plan a protest that would convince Kennedy of the vital need for such a law. They decided to hold it in Birmingham, Alabama, which had the reputation of being the most segregated city in the country. The Ku Klux Klan was extremely active in

Birmingham's Public Safety Commissioner Eugene "Bull" Connor was known for his poor treatment of blacks. He got his nickname because his voice was so loud, it sounded as if he were talking through a bullhorn.

Birmingham. Klansmen made a habit of bombing African American homes and churches. They had destroyed so many that the city's nickname was "Bombingham."

Another reason for selecting Birmingham was the city's Public Safety Commissioner Eugene "Bull" Connor, who was notorious for going out of his way to arrest and abuse blacks. If the protest in Birmingham was reported in the media, the American people would see Connor in action. They hoped that the public outcry would force the president to act.

Project C

The Birmingham demonstration was called Project C—for confrontation. The SCLC planned to hold sit-ins at the white-only lunch counters and "colored" restrooms at five of Birmingham's largest department stores. There would also be marches and demonstrations to dissuade people from shopping at the stores.

Project C began on April 3, the height of the Easter shopping season. Birmingham had just elected a new mayor, Albert Boutwell, and Bull Connor, one of the three commissioners who had previously run the city, was out of office. In view of Connor's defeat, the city's business leaders asked King to call off the project

The Birmingham demonstration was called Project C—for confrontation.

and give Boutwell a chance to work on Birmingham's racial problems. King refused. As far as he was concerned, Boutwell was "just a dignified Bull Connor." Besides, the country needed to be reminded that racism was an ongoing problem in the American South.

Project C was just getting underway when Bull Connor came up with a plan to remain in office. He filed a lawsuit asking that he and the other defeated commissioners be allowed to serve out the terms they had been elected to before the mayoral form of government was adopted. Until the court could decide whether Boutwell or Connor and the other commissioners were the legal government of Birmingham, the city had two governments. No one knew which one was in charge, so municipal business came to a standstill. The only thing everyone agreed on was that public safety had to be maintained. Hence, Connor retained control of the police force.

A Slow Start

During the first week of Project C, Bull Connor made 102 arrests. After that, the number dwindled. The majority of Birmingham's blacks did not want to demonstrate. Some feared retaliation from the Ku Klux Klan. Others were afraid of being sent to jail, where they were sure to be beaten by white guards. For the next few days, Birmingham was so quiet that the reporters, who had come to town expecting a front-page story, were ready to pack up and go home.

King was on the verge of calling off the project when Bull Connor got an injunction from an Alabama state court that forbade the SCLC leaders from encouraging or engaging in demonstrations of any kind. The injunction gave King an opportunity to revive Project C. If he defied it by leading a protest, Connor would have to arrest him. The story would be at the top of the evening news.

King called a press conference to announce that he was going to lead a march on Good Friday, April 12. "I am prepared to go to jail and stay as long as necessary," he said.

For Christians, the significance of the day was hard to miss. "Almost two thousand years ago, Christ died on the Cross for us," Ralph Abernathy declared. "Tomorrow we will take it up for our people, and die if necessary."

On Friday morning, with the protest only hours away, King and his staff received word that the SCLC was short of funds. King had promised to bail out the demonstrators who had been arrested the previous week, but he needed money to do it. Several of his aides wanted him to put Project C on hold and go on a speaking tour to raise funds.

Jailed Again

King vetoed the suggestion. "I don't know whether I can raise money to get people out of jail," he said. "I do know that I can go to jail with them."

That afternoon, King led some fifty people out of SCLC's Birmingham office and began walking toward City Hall. A few minutes later, Connor's officers dragged the marchers into police vans and took them to jail. King's arrest was front-page news, and the nation's attention became riveted on Birmingham.

Coretta Scott King was distressed to hear of her husband's jailing. She had given birth to their fourth child, Bernice, only

King being taken to the Birmingham jail after defying an injunction against leading a protest. King wore a work shirt and blue jeans that day. It was the first time most of his followers had seen him in anything but a business suit.

two weeks earlier. Martin always managed to get in touch with her when he was jailed. This time, three days passed without any news. When Easter Sunday arrived and there was still no word, Coretta called the White House. President Kennedy returned her call the next day. He assured her that her husband was all right and that he was working to get him released. Shortly after that, King started receiving better treatment. He was released from solitary confinement and allowed to take a shower and place a call to Coretta.

Eight days later, King and Abernathy posted bail. King explained that their trial for defying the Alabama state court injunction was to begin in two days and they had to consult with their lawyers. Two days later, the men appeared in court and were found guilty of contempt. When they told the judge that they planned to appeal the sentence, he allowed them to remain free.

While Martin Luther King, Jr., was in jail, eight of Birmingham's white clergymen published an open letter in the *Birmingham News*. They criticized King and called the SCLC protests "unwise and untimely." The clergymen asked the city's blacks not to support them.

King responded to the clergymen with a 6,500-word letter written in the margins of the newspaper and on whatever scraps of paper he could find. His lawyer smuggled it out of his cell. "Letter from Birmingham City Jail" was later published as a pamphlet by a Quaker organization, the American Friends Service Committee. It was reprinted many times and became one of the principal documents of the civil rights movement.

The Children's Demonstration

During the week King was in jail, the demonstrations in Birmingham came to a halt. All the blacks who were willing to

"Letter from Birmingham City Jail"

King's letter to the eight white Birmingham clergymen was particularly critical of the clergymen's use of the word "untimely."

"Perhaps it is easy for those who have never felt the stinging darts of segregation to say, 'Wait,' " he wrote. "But . . . when you have to concoct an answer for a five-year-old son asking in agonizing pathos: 'Daddy, why do white people treat colored folks so mean?'; when you take a cross-country drive and find it necessary to sleep night after night in the uncomfortable corners of your automobile because no motel will accept you; when you are humiliated day in and day out by nagging signs reading 'white' and 'colored'; . . . then you will understand why we find it difficult to wait . . ."

King also criticized the clergymen's statement commending the Birmingham police force for keeping order and preventing violence.

"I wish you had commended the Negro sit-inners and demonstrators of Birmingham for their sublime courage, their willingness to suffer and their amazing discipline in the midst of great provocation."

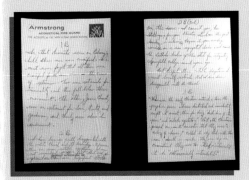

This photocopy of Martin Luther King, Jr.'s "Letter from Birmingham City Jail" was part of a collection of King's papers that was put up for auction in 2006. The collection was bought by a group of Atlanta residents who donated it to Morehouse College.

Birmingham police officers lead black school children to jail for protesting against segregation. A police captain tried to talk the younger children out of marching, but they assured him they knew what they were doing.

demonstrate had already been arrested. One of King's aides, James Bevel, came up with the idea of replacing the adults with high school and elementary school students.

King disapproved of Bevel's plan. He was afraid that some of the children might get hurt; but Bevel talked him into it. The aide had already lined up an army of young people ranging in age from six to eighteen. He told them to be ready to march on Thursday, May 2.

That day over one thousand children stayed home from school and gathered at the Sixteenth Street Baptist Church. King spoke to them briefly. Then they marched out of the church, singing and clapping. Their version of "We Shall Overcome" sounded more like a ragtime tune than a hymn. The march continued for the next four hours. When Bull Connor's police arrested them, they knelt and prayed. By the end of the day, over nine hundred children had been arrested. Connor quickly ran out of police vans and had to round up a fleet of school buses to take them to jail.

Bevel held a second march the next day. This time the marchers encountered firefighters armed with fire hoses. The force of the water slammed the young people against trees and parked cars. Police dogs broke up the crowd that had gathered along the street to cheer the young people on.

The television shots of black children being assaulted with fire hoses, and police dogs unleashed on innocent bystanders horrified the American public. They flooded the White House with letters and phone calls begging the president to intervene. Because no federal laws were being violated, Kennedy did not

The hoses Birmingham's firefighters trained on demonstrators were powerful enough to strip the bark off trees. One blast of water knocked a little girl to the ground and sent her tumbling down the street.

have the authority to act. Instead, he sent Assistant Attorney General Burke Marshall to Birmingham with instructions to resolve the situation.

Marshall arrived to find the city still without a working government. Although Albert Boutwell had been sworn in as mayor, Bull Connor's lawsuit was still pending. Until it could be settled, the city was being run by a coalition of white businessmen.

By this time, Project C had taken on a new life. The assaults on the school children had enraged Birmingham's blacks and they rushed to join the protests. As the size of the demonstrations increased, the white businessmen became concerned about an outbreak of violence. They hastened to integrate the lunch counters, restrooms, and water fountains at the stores that had been picketed and promised to make them hire blacks as salespeople and clerical workers. In return, King cancelled Project C.

An Uneasy Peace

When King's agreement with the businessmen was announced, Bull Connor denounced him as a "rabble-rousing Negro" and urged the city's whites to boycott the stores that had given in to his demands. The following night, more than a thousand Ku Klux Klansmen gathered outside the city and heard the Imperial Wizard of the Alabama Klan denounce both sides in the negotiations.

That same night, the motel where King and his aides were staying, and the home of King's brother, A. D., the pastor of a Birmingham church, were bombed. A crowd of blacks converged on both sites and a riot erupted. By the time it ended, thirty-five blacks and five whites had been hurt and seven stores had been set on fire.

This May 1963 photo shows the wreckage left by the bomb explosion at the Gaston Motel, where King and his associates were staying in Birmingham.

Fearful that the riots might spread to other cities, President Kennedy made a speech in which he declared, "This government will do whatever must be done to preserve the lives of its citizens and uphold the law of the land . . ."

Kennedy's speech calmed things down. The tensions were further eased on May 23 when the Alabama Supreme Court ruled against Bull Connor. Albert Boutwell and the city council that had been elected with him were the legal government in Birmingham. Boutwell hastened to approve the settlement between the businessmen and the SCLC. For the first time in weeks, Birmingham dropped out of the headlines.

> *"This government will do whatever must be done to preserve the lives of its citizens and uphold the law of the land . . ."*

The Ku Klux Klan

The Ku Klux Klan was founded in 1866 by a group of Southerners who wanted to preserve white supremacy after the emancipation of the slaves. The name was derived from the Greek word for "circle" or "band." Klan members met in secret and wore white robes, tall white hats, and masks to disguise their identities.

A Ku Klux Klan parade in Washington, D.C., in 1926. This revived version of the Klan, which was organized in 1915, was opposed to Jews, Catholics, and immigrants, as well as blacks. The second Klan died out in the late 1920s.

Klansmen rode through the countryside at night, flogging, shooting, and lynching blacks and burning their homes at will. The violence became so widespread that President Ulysses S. Grant sent federal troops to abolish the organization. Its leaders were arrested and imprisoned, and by 1872 the Ku Klux Klan had ceased to exist.

When *Brown v. Board of Education of Topeka* threatened the South's long-standing laws against integration, a new version of the Klan appeared. Most of its members were poor white men who lived in the rural areas of Mississippi and Alabama. Like their predecessors, they wore white robes and hoods and adopted the flaming cross as their symbol. Blacks who showed an interest in integration were likely to have their homes bombed or to be beaten or killed by Klansmen.

CHAPTER 9

The March on Washington

There will be neither rest nor tranquility in America until the Negro is granted his citizenship rights.

The awful scene in Birmingham proved to be a turning point in the civil rights movement. More and more people began showing up at King's speeches, making donations to the SCLC, and participating in civil rights marches. A high percentage of them were white. President Kennedy could feel the mounting pressure to do something about the issue, but his advisers warned him to proceed cautiously.

On June 11, 1963, less than three weeks after Birmingham quieted down, Governor George Wallace of Alabama defied a federal court order to admit two black students to the University of Alabama. Wallace was so fiercely opposed to integration that he stood at

Governor George Wallace confronts Deputy Attorney General Nicholas Katzenbach (right foreground) at the University of Alabama. When Katzenbach failed to persuade Wallace to integrate the school, President Kennedy sent the National Guard to make him obey.

the door of the school's administration building to keep the students from entering.

The governor's action was an obvious violation of the law. President Kennedy placed the Alabama National Guard under federal control and sent them to the university. When their commanding officer told Wallace to step aside on orders from the president of the United States, the governor withdrew. The University of Alabama became the last state university in the country to be integrated.

George Wallace's defiance of a federal court order coming so soon after Bull Connor's brutality in Birmingham spurred Kennedy into action. That evening, he announced to the nation that he would send a civil rights bill to Congress.

A March for Civil Rights

Although the surprise announcement convinced King that the president was committed to the bill, he felt that a mass protest in Washington was needed to remind Congress of its importance. King consulted with his friend Stanley Levison in New York, who told him that A. Philip Randolph, who had organized the 1957 Prayer Pilgrimage for Freedom, was already planning a march. Levison was sure that Randolph would want King to join him.

Early in July of 1963, Randolph called a meeting of the nation's major civil rights leaders. They voted to hold a march on August 28. John F. Kennedy was not happy to hear about their plans. He invited them to a meeting at the White House. Although he understood their desire to see the civil rights bill passed, Kennedy told them, he didn't think a march on Washington was the way to do it.

"We want success in the Congress," Kennedy told the civil rights leaders, "not a big show on the Capitol."

George C. Wallace (1919–1998)

George Corley Wallace was born in Alabama in 1919. When he ran in the 1958 primary, hoping to become the Democratic candidate for governor, he was considered a moderate on race. After losing to a segregationist, he changed his views and became a staunch segregationist himself.

Wallace won the 1962 election for governor by a huge majority. When a state law prevented him from running for another term, his wife, Lurleen Wallace, ran in his place and won. After the law on term limits was repealed, Wallace won a second four-year term in 1970 and a third in 1974.

An undated portrait of George C. Wallace, governor of Alabama. After being a staunch segregationist for several decades, Wallace eventually changed his position and said that he wholeheartedly supported integration.

In 1964 and 1968, Wallace ran in the Democratic presidential primaries, campaigning largely against blacks. During his third run in 1972, Wallace was shot by a seriously disturbed man and left paralyzed from the waist down. Although he entered the 1976 primary, questions about his health, combined with Southern support for Georgia Governor Jimmy Carter, convinced him to withdraw from the race.

When Wallace ran for governor for the fourth time in 1982, he had had a change of heart. He apologized for his earlier stand against integration and he won the election with the overwhelming support of Alabama's blacks. In 1986, Wallace announced his retirement from public life. He died in 1998.

Martin Luther King, Jr., respectfully disagreed. He hoped the march—officially called The March on Washington for Jobs and Freedom—would make the entire country aware of the need for civil rights legislation. Kennedy conceded the point but he still thought the march was ill-timed. "Frankly," King replied, "I have never engaged in a direct-action movement that did not seem ill-timed. Some people thought Birmingham was ill-timed."

Kennedy dropped his objections to the march when he learned that several influential white organizations were sending delegations to it. The list included the American Jewish Congress, the National Conference of Catholics for Interracial Justice, the National Council of Churches, and the United Auto Workers Union, one of the largest labor unions in the country.

Shortly after dawn on the morning of August 28, the marchers began pouring into the capital. The civil rights leaders had been hoping to attract 100,000 people. They were stunned when some 250,000 showed up.

On August 28, 1963, about 250,000 marchers gathered on the Mall in Washington, D.C. More than 30 special trains and 20,000 chartered buses brought the participants to the capital.

While the marchers were assembling on the grounds of the Washington Monument, King and the other civil rights leaders made the rounds on Capitol Hill. They met with every congressman and senator who was willing to see them. Their message was simple: Please pass the bill.

Around noon, the crowd that had gathered at the Washington Monument formed into ranks and began walking toward the Lincoln Memorial. Black soprano Camilla Williams sang "The Star Spangled Banner," the Roman Catholic Archbishop of Washington, the Reverend Patrick O'Boyle, gave an opening prayer, and A. Philip Randolph delivered the opening address. The program included speeches by prominent African Americans, but the last and most impressive—the speaker everyone had been waiting for—was Martin Luther King, Jr.

I Have a Dream

King had prepared a solemn address for the occasion. "Five score years ago," he began, "a great American in whose symbolic shadow we stand today, signed the Emancipation Proclamation. This momentous decree came as a great beacon light of hope to millions of Negro slaves who had been seared in the flames of withering injustice. It came as a joyous daybreak to end the long night of their captivity."

Martin Luther King, Jr., is shown delivering his famous "I have a dream" speech. Although the speech was based on one of his favorite sermons, he forgot some of the words and had to make up new ones as he went along.

The SCLC leader spoke in this elaborate style for several minutes. Then he sensed that his listeners were tired of formal speeches. Adopting a more relaxed tone, he launched into one of his favorite sermons. ". . .Even though we face the difficulties of today and tomorrow," he said, "I still have a dream. It is a dream deeply rooted in the American meaning of its creed, 'We hold these truths to be self-evident, that all men are created equal . . .' "

At various points in the speech, King repeated the phrase "I have a dream." Among the most familiar lines is, "I have a dream that my four little children will one day live in a nation where they will not be judged by the color of their skin but by the content of their character."

The speech captured the joyful mood of the day. When King finished, the crowd erupted into cheers. The volunteers assigned to keep order had to form a circle around him to keep him from being crushed by his admirers.

President John F. Kennedy had been concerned that the march would erupt into violence. He had placed four thousand troops on alert and had fifteen thousand paratroopers standing by in North Carolina. The troops were not needed. As one journalist noted, "The sweetness and patience of the crowd may have set some sort of national high-water mark in mass decency."

Following the successful March on Washington, President John F. Kennedy met with leaders of the march, which was one of the few times blacks and whites, Protestants, Jews, and Catholics joined together to support a cause. Martin Luther King, Jr., is second from the left.

The president had invited the black leaders to a reception at the White House after the March. Kennedy was pleased that the day had gone so well. He went out of his way to congratulate King on his speech. When the civil rights leader shook the president's hand, he felt confident that Kennedy would do everything possible to see that the civil rights bill became law.

Desegregating Hearts

Although the leaders of the country's major civil rights organizations presented a united front in public, there were a number of rifts amongst them. Roy Wilkins, the executive secretary of the NAACP, disapproved of King's direct action campaigns. The NAACP believed in achieving civil rights through court decisions such as *Brown v. Board of Education of Topeka*.

In a photo taken between 1960 and 1965, Roy Wilkins, executive secretary of the NAACP, shakes hands with Martin Luther King, Jr. Relations between the two men became strained after the SCLC threatened to displace the NAACP as the country's leading civil rights organization.

Wilkins regularly reminded King that an NAACP lawsuit— not King's leadership of the MIA—had ended the Montgomery bus boycott. He liked to needle King by pointing out that his marches and demonstrations had not desegregated a single classroom in Albany or Birmingham.

"In fact, Martin," Wilkins once said, "if you have desegregated *anything* by your efforts, kindly enlighten me."

"I guess the only thing I've desegregated so far is a few human hearts," King replied.

CHAPTER 10

Tragedies and Triumphs

I accept this [Nobel] prize on behalf of all men who love peace and brotherhood.

Less than three weeks after the March on Washington, the Ku Klux Klan set off a dynamite blast at the Sixteenth Street Baptist Church in Birmingham. Four black girls, who were attending a Bible class, were killed. King could not help feeling guilty about their deaths. He knew the blast was revenge for Project C. He did his best to console the girls' families and preached at the joint funeral that was held for three of the victims.

Later that fall, President John F. Kennedy was assassinated in Dallas. King was shocked and saddened by the president's death. He could not help thinking that something similar would happen to him. "I don't think I'm going to live to reach forty," he told Coretta.

"I don't think I'm going to live to reach forty," he told Coretta.

King went to Washington for Kennedy's funeral. He found a very different city from the one he had visited in August. The streets were full of sad faces and the White House was draped in black. King had been disappointed in John F. Kennedy for taking so long to recognize the need for a federal civil rights law, but at least he had finally done something. King could not help wondering what would happen to the bill now.

Passage of the Civil Rights Bill

Despite his Southern roots, Kennedy's successor, Vice President Lyndon B. Johnson, was sympathetic to civil rights. In his first address to Congress, on November 27, 1963, Johnson told the legislators, "No memorial oration or eulogy could more eloquently honor President Kennedy's memory than the earliest possible passage of the civil rights bill for which he fought so long."

The House of Representatives passed the bill on February 10. From there it went to the Senate.

While the Civil Rights Act was being debated in the Senate, King was leading a protest against white-only motels and restaurants in St. Augustine, Florida. The city proved to be more lawless than Birmingham. Members of the Ku Klux Klan hurled sulfuric acid at the demonstrators. The police used cattle prods—poles that deliver a painful electric shock—to evict sixteen rabbis and their black guests from a restaurant. Dozens of blacks were beaten. Many were seriously injured. One night, Klansmen fired on the beach house where King was staying. Luckily, he was making a speech in Los Angeles at the time.

African American demonstrators were arrested while trying to integrate the Monson Motor Lodge in St. Augustine, Florida. They are shown being taken to jail in a police wagon, while a guard armed with a club sits in the rear of the wagon.

The protests in St. Augustine were notable for the number of whites who joined them. Among those arrested were the Reverend William Sloane Coffin, chaplain of Yale University, and Mrs. Malcolm Peabody, the seventy-two-year-old mother of the governor of Massachusetts.

Finally, on June 19, after two more months of quarreling over the bill, the Senate passed it, seventy-three to twenty-seven. On July 2, King was among the distinguished guests who gathered in the East Room of the White House to watch President Lyndon B. Johnson sign the Civil Rights Act of 1964 into law.

With Martin Luther King, Jr., looking on, President Lyndon B. Johnson signs the Civil Rights Act of 1964 in the East Room of the White House. Johnson signed 72 copies of the law and gave them to his guests as souvenirs.

The Civil Rights Act of 1964

The Civil Rights Act of 1964 was the most sweeping civil rights legislation in the history of the country. It put an end to Jim Crow laws, making segregation illegal in parks, playgrounds, libraries, and similar public facilities. It also forbade discrimination in places of public accommodation, such as restaurants, hotels, motels, and theaters. In addition, the bill outlawed discrimination in employment and education and set up a Commission on Equal Employment Opportunity to deal with bias in the workplace. The Civil Rights Act of 1964 applied not only to blacks but to other victims of discrimination, including women.

Initially, segregationists resisted the new law, but the federal government was determined to enforce it. In time, the resistance died away and integration in public institutions became a fact of life.

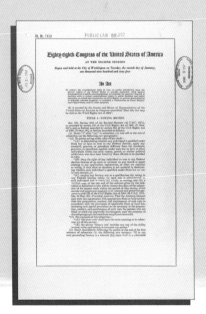

The first page of Public Law 88-352, better known as the Civil Rights Act of 1964. Johnson considered the bill so important, he had his signing of it televised.

King Receives the Peace Prize

On an October weekend in 1964, King delivered four speeches in cities on the East Coast and then flew to St. Louis to give two more on Monday. He returned home exhausted. On Tuesday, his doctor had him admitted to the hospital for a much-needed rest. The next morning, Coretta called him at the hospital.

"Martin!" she said. "You've won the Nobel Peace Prize!"

King could hardly believe it. "For a while I thought it was a dream," he said later. "And then I realized it was true!"

The prize had been given to King for his leadership in the fight for civil rights and his commitment to nonviolence. Without this principle, the committee declared, King's "demonstrations and marches could easily have become violent and ended with the spilling of blood."

President Johnson and Attorney General Robert Kennedy were quick to congratulate King on the award. On December 4, Martin and Coretta King flew to Oslo, Norway, with a large party

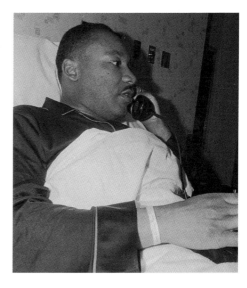

While being treated for exhaustion at Atlanta's St. Joseph's Infirmary (now St. Joseph's Hospital), King receives a phone call congratulating him on winning the 1964 Nobel Peace Prize. Previous winners from the U.S. were Presidents Theodore Roosevelt and Woodrow Wilson and the pioneer social worker Jane Addams.

Martin Luther King, Jr., shaking hands with Norway's Crown Prince Harald and King Olav at the Nobel Prize ceremonies. King accepted the award on behalf of the civil rights movement for its efforts "to establish a reign of freedom and a rule of justice."

of family and friends. They made a brief stopover in London, where King met with members of Parliament and spoke from the pulpit of St. Paul's Cathedral. He had the distinction of being the first non-**Anglican** to preach at the famous church.

On December 10, King stood in the marble hall at Oslo University and accepted the Nobel Peace Prize before an audience of several hundred people. The prize also included a cash award of $54,600, which King donated to the civil rights movement.

More Work to Be Done

Between the passage of the Civil Rights Act and the presentation of the Nobel Peace Prize, 1964 had been a good year for King. At the same time, he knew there was more work to be done. The Civil Rights Act did not include a provision for voting rights, which were routinely denied to blacks in the South.

Although African Americans had a constitutional right to vote, segregationist politicians in many states—particularly in Mississippi and Alabama—made it all but impossible for them to become registered voters. The politicians knew that if the large numbers of blacks in their states could vote, they would drive the segregationists out of office.

Most blacks did not even attempt to register. The registration offices were open at inconvenient hours, and the registrars specialized in insulting black applicants. Perhaps the worst part of trying to register, however, was the long and confusing literacy tests that prospective voters had to take. Southern blacks, who were seldom well educated, found them impossible to pass—which was exactly what the segregationists intended.

On their way home from Oslo, Martin and Coretta King stopped at the White House to see President Lyndon B. Johnson. In the course of their visit, King asked Johnson to send Congress a voting rights bill. President Johnson said no. He felt that one civil rights bill was enough for a while. There was a limit to how much the South would put up with. King did not argue with the president, but he promised himself that his next project would be a voting rights drive.

In an effort to get blacks to register and vote, this black child wears a sign that says, "I'm too young to vote—What is your excuse?" Even before the start of the civil rights movement, the NAACP conducted voter registration drives in black ghettos around the country.

The Nobel Peace Prize

Dr. Alfred Nobel, the Swedish industrialist who invented dynamite, established the Nobel Prizes, which are given for achievements in physics, chemistry, physiology, medicine, literature, economics, and peace. Nobel stipulated in his will that all the prizes were to be presented in Sweden except the Peace Prize, which was to be awarded in Norway. The award ceremonies are held on December 10, the anniversary of his death in 1896.

In addition to a cash award, Nobel Peace Prize winners receive a gold medal with Alfred Nobel's image on its face. The medal, which was designed by the Norwegian sculptor Gustav Vigeland, was first presented in 1902.

The reverse side of the Nobel Peace Prize medal shows a group of three men forming a fraternal bond. The Latin inscription, *Pro pace et fraternitate gentium*, is translated as "For the peace and brotherhood of men."

At thirty-five years of age, Martin Luther King, Jr., was the youngest person ever to receive the Nobel Peace Prize and only the third black. The previous blacks to be honored were Dr. Ralph Bunche, for his work as undersecretary of the United Nations, and Chief Albert Luthuli of South Africa, for his campaign of passive resistance against apartheid laws—the South African version of Jim Crow laws.

CHAPTER 11

From Selma to Montgomery

Our cry to the state of Alabama is a simple one:
"Give us the ballot!"

On January 2, 1965, Martin Luther King, Jr., stood before some seven hundred people in Brown Chapel African Methodist Episcopal Church in Selma, the county seat of Dallas County, Alabama. He asked them to join a SCLC-sponsored project aimed at forcing the federal government to pass a law that would prevent African Americans from being deprived of their right to vote. The project would begin with a series of mass marches at the Dallas County Courthouse, where the Board of Registrars had its offices. The marches would take place on the first and third Thursdays of every month, the only two days the offices were open.

King points to Selma, Alabama, on a map in the SCLC's office in Atlanta. When the voting rights campaign began, the city had 15,000 blacks of voting age but only 156 were registered voters.

Dallas County Sheriff Jim Clark used a billy club and an electric cattle prod to intimidate demonstrators demanding the right to register to vote. Clark forced the protestors to stand in an alley behind the county courthouse.

Marching for Voter Rights

The SCLC campaign began on January 18. Four hundred demonstrators, led by King and John Lewis, the national chairman of SNCC, marched to the courthouse to register as voters. The sheriff of Dallas County, Jim Clark, herded them into an alley behind the building and would not let them inside. The next day, King and Lewis led another band of demonstrators to the courthouse to protest Clark's refusal to let them register the day before. When they disobeyed his order to stand in the alley, the sheriff lost his temper. He grabbed one woman and began shoving her down the street. A picture of the incident appeared in the *Washington Post* and the *New York Times*—two of the country's leading newspapers.

A week later, about 450 African Americans held a night march in the neighboring town of Marion. Minutes after it began, the streetlights went out and a mob of white supremacists began attacking the marchers. A young black man, Jimmy Lee Jackson, was shot by a state trooper. He died seven days later.

The civil rights protestors decided to commemorate Jackson's death by staging a march from Marion to the state capital in Montgomery. They planned to knock on the capitol door and present their request for voting rights to Governor George Wallace in person.

The march was scheduled for Sunday, March 7. The route would take the demonstrators through Selma to the Edmund Pettus Bridge, which spanned the Alabama River. From there, they would follow Route 80 to Montgomery. The fifty-four-mile march would take four or five days and was bound to be extensively covered in the press.

Deaths Along the Way

King was in Atlanta that Sunday conducting services at Ebenezer Baptist Church. One of his aides, Hosea Williams, led the march in his place. John Lewis marched at his side. The protest went smoothly until the marchers crossed the Edmund Pettus Bridge and found a wall of Alabama state troopers on the other side. Their commanding officer gave the demonstrators two minutes to disband and go home. Hosea Williams tried to speak to the officer, but the man curtly informed him that there was nothing to discuss.

Seconds later, the troopers began shoving the demonstrators. Many were knocked to the ground and beaten with nightsticks. Another detachment of troopers fired tear gas. Mounted troopers charged the crowd on horseback. Television cameras captured the clash on film and a Sunday afternoon television program was interrupted to show the footage. The nation was appalled.

That day became known as Bloody Sunday. In response to

That day became known as Bloody Sunday.

Alabama state troopers attacking demonstrators on Bloody Sunday, March 7, 1965. SNCC chairman John Lewis (on the ground, center) was among the dozens of blacks who were hurt in the assault. Lewis had to be hospitalized for head injuries.

the violence, King invited white clergymen from around the country to join a ministers' march to Montgomery two days later. King asked U.S. District Court Judge Frank M. Johnson, Jr., to issue an injunction forbidding Governor Wallace from interfering with the marchers.

The judge could not review the matter right away, so the march was postponed for a few days. Confident that Johnson would grant King's request, most of the white clergymen stayed on in Selma. One evening, three ministers were leaving a restaurant when a man emerged from the darkness and bashed one of them on the head with a club. The minister, a Bostonian named James Reeb, died two days later.

The second death threw Governor Wallace into a panic. Alabama already looked bad. The march would make things worse. Wallace flew to Washington over the weekend and pleaded with President Johnson to get King to call off the march.

Martin Luther King, Jr., and Ralph Abernathy lead a march of religious leaders down the main street of Selma. The march was held in memory of minister James Reeb, who was killed by a white supremacist.

After turning the governor down, Johnson took him into the Rose Garden for a presidential press conference. The main topic was Bloody Sunday. Johnson called the events in Selma "an American tragedy" and announced that he would send a bill to Congress that would "strike down all restrictions used to deny the people the right to vote."

On Monday, Johnson delivered a speech to Congress. He asked the legislators to pass a bill that would give African Americans the voting rights they were entitled to. "Their cause must be our cause, too," the president said. "Because it's not just Negroes, but it's really all of us who must overcome the crippling legacy of bigotry and injustice. And we *shall* overcome."

King watched the speech on television with several of his aides. One of them, C. T. Vivian, recalled that when Johnson said, "We shall overcome," they all cheered. Vivian looked over at King, who was sitting very quietly in an easy chair, and saw a tear running down his cheek.

The March to Montgomery

Two days after President Johnson's address to Congress, Judge Johnson ruled that the SCLC had "a legal and constitutional right to march from Selma to Montgomery."

The march was scheduled for Sunday, March 21. When Governor Wallace declined to provide police protection for the marchers, President Johnson placed the Alabama National Guard under federal control. He sent them to the scene along with troops from the U.S. Army and a sizable contingent of FBI agents and federal marshals.

On March 21, a racially mixed crowd of about four thousand people marched out of Brown Chapel with King at the head of the line. He was flanked by his fellow Nobel Prize winner, Undersecretary-General of the United Nations Dr. Ralph Bunche, and Rabbi Abraham Heschel of the Jewish Theological Seminary in New York.

On March 21, 1965, the March from Selma to Montgomery began. From left to right: Ralph Abernathy, Martin Luther King, Jr., Dr. Ralph Bunche, and Rabbi Abraham Heschel lead the way.

The march was no longer just for ministers. People from all over the country, of all different ages and backgrounds, joined in. Some of them walked the whole way. Others marched for a day or two to show their support. At night, the out-of-towners slept in oversize tents that were set up along the highway. Volunteers from the SCLC office in Selma delivered their meals.

The SCLC had heard a rumor that white supremacists planned to assassinate Martin Luther King, Jr., as he entered Montgomery. One of King's aides, Andrew Young, rounded up about a half dozen black men who had the same build as King and wore the same kind of dark blue suits. Young put them at the head of the march as decoys.

Participants in the march from Selma to Montgomery take time out to rest. The SCLC provided food, water, shelter, and medical care for the marchers. The most common ailment was blistered feet.

"I figured since we couldn't stop him from marching," he said, "we just had to believe that it was true when white folks said that we all looked alike."

Twenty-five thousand people completed the final six miles of the March to Montgomery. They arrived on March 25. King strode to the top of the capitol steps with Rosa Parks at his side. There were speeches from Parks, Ralph Bunche, Roy Wilkins, John Lewis, and, of course, Martin Luther King, Jr. When they ended, King and the other speakers approached the entrance to the capitol with a petition for Governor Wallace. A line of state troopers blocked the door. One of them announced that the governor wasn't in. Undeterred, the blacks remained at the entrance until one of Wallace's secretaries appeared and took the petition.

Alabama's State Capitol

Alabama's state capitol in Montgomery is a white stone building with stately pillars and a large dome. Montgomery was the first capital of the Confederacy. A commemorative star on the top step to the right of the door marks the spot where Jefferson Davis stood to take his oath of office as president of the Confederate States of America. Montgomery was the seat of the Confederate government from February to May of 1861, when the capital was moved to Richmond, Virginia.

By coincidence, the Dexter Avenue Baptist Church, where Martin Luther King, Jr., was pastor when the Montgomery bus boycott began, is just across the square from the capitol. The civil rights marchers passed it on their way to present their petition to Governor George Wallace.

Tragedy Strikes

The demonstrators had been told to leave Montgomery as soon as the march was over. Roving bands of white supremacists might be waiting to attack them. The SCLC had recruited volunteers to drive the marchers back to Selma. Among them was a white woman named Viola Liuzzo. She had seen the pictures of Bloody Sunday on television and had gone to Selma to help.

This undated photograph shows civil rights worker Viola Liuzzo and her husband and children. Liuzzo's husband called her a champion of the underdog. "She thought people's rights were being violated in Selma," he said, "and she had to do something about it . . ."

Liuzzo and another volunteer, a nineteen-year-old black man named Leroy Moton, had already dropped off five marchers at Brown Chapel. They were headed back to Montgomery to pick up a second load of passengers. As Liuzzo and Moton were driving along Route 80, a car tried to force them off the road. Another car with four Ku Klux Klan members inside pulled up beside them. One of the four men shot Liuzzo in the face, killing her instantly. Her car veered into a ditch and crashed against a fence.

Another Klansmen climbed down to make sure the gunman had hit his mark. Although Leroy Moton was covered with blood, the bullets had missed him. He pretended to be dead, and the Klansman left. As soon as the men drove off, Moton scrambled up to the highway and flagged down a truck carrying some of the demonstrators.

The day after Viola Liuzzo's murder, the FBI arrested four Ku Klux Klan members for the crime. Three of them were tried for murder in an Alabama state court. The fourth, who had been working as an informant for the FBI, was not charged.

Despite overwhelming evidence to the contrary, the three men were found not guilty.

Later that year, the federal government indicted the three Klansmen on charges of depriving Liuzzo of her civil rights. All three were found guilty and given the maximum sentence of ten years.

The death of Violet Liuzzo intensified public support for the Voting Rights Act. The bill passed the Senate on May 26, 1965, by a vote of seventy-seven to nineteen. The House was slower to give its approval. After five weeks of debate, it was finally passed on July 9. On August 6, President Johnson signed the bill into law with King and Rosa Parks along with other civil rights leaders in attendance.

CHAPTER 12

A Shift in the Black Struggle

What we now need is a new kind of Selma or Birmingham to dramatize the economic plight of the Negro and compel the government to act.

The March to Montgomery was the high point of the civil rights movement. It was also the last time it attracted substantial support from whites. A new generation of African Americans was beginning to question King's commitment to nonviolence. Many of them were poor blacks in Northern cities. They thought he spent too much time hobnobbing with white people to understand their problems. They also resented the fact that, despite his many eloquent speeches about civil rights, they were still trapped in rat-infested ghettos and could not find decent jobs.

The anger of inner-city blacks became evident in the summer of 1965 when a riot erupted in a Los Angeles slum known as Watts.

The Watts Riot

On the night of August 11, a white police officer stopped a black driver who appeared to be drunk. The driver, twenty-one-year-old Marquette Frye, was with his brother, Ronald. As the officer was talking to Frye, a crowd gathered. A few minutes later, Frye's mother showed up

In August of 1965, race riots erupted in Watts, a poor area of Los Angeles, and many stores were looted. In this August 13 photograph, looters are shown carrying clothing and boxes from a store in the area. Most of the stores were later set on fire. The fires raged out of control for hours because the rioters attacked the firefighters who tried to put them out.

and began berating the policeman. The officer called for backup, and a second officer arrived on the scene. There was a struggle, and the police arrested all three Fryes.

When the onlookers protested the arrests, one of the officers threatened them with his nightstick. The crowd became unruly, and additional police were called. By ten o'clock that night, more than twenty police cars had blocked off the streets that led in and out of Watts. As news of the barricade spread, the crowd grew larger and more hostile.

People started throwing rocks and bottles, and the turmoil escalated into a riot. By the time it ended six days later, thirty-four people were dead and over a thousand had been injured. Approximately six hundred buildings had been looted and set on fire. Almost all of them were stores and businesses owned by whites. The total damage was estimated at $100 million.

King visited Watts and toured the wreckage. When he tried to make a speech in the devastated neighborhood, he was interrupted by enraged residents. One man yelled, "Get out of here, Dr. King! We don't want you." A woman shouted that Parker and Yorty—referring to the police chief and the mayor of Los Angeles—should come to Watts and see the terrible conditions they lived in.

The crowd eventually calmed down and allowed King to speak. Later he held a meeting with Police Chief William Parker and Mayor Sam Yorty and mentioned several ways in which they could address the complaints of the ghetto-dwellers. The two men rejected them all.

In King's opinion, Yorty and Parker were as racist as any city officials he had met in the South. Although King told reporters that he could not find "any statesmanship and creative leadership" in Los Angeles, he also admitted, "We as Negro leaders—and I include myself—have failed to take the civil rights movement to the masses of the people."

Black Power

Some of the anger that had triggered the riot in Watts had already surfaced among members of SNCC. Many of them had been beaten by white supremacists during the Freedom Rides and lunch counter sit-ins. They had also participated in voter registration drives in rural Mississippi where three of their co-workers had been savagely murdered by Ku Klux Klansmen. Enduring such hatred without striking back made no sense to them.

SNCC chairman Stokely Carmichael addresses a crowd at the University of California-Berkeley in October of 1966. Carmichael's militant attitude caused some people to start calling the organization the Nonstudent Violent Coordinating Committee.

In 1966, SNCC elected a fiery young man named Stokely Carmichael as their national chairman. Carmichael adopted the slogan "Black Power" and called on blacks to claim their rights and build their own organizations so they would not have to depend on whites for help. He did not actually advocate violence, but he left no doubt that he considered it an appropriate way to deal with white oppression.

Although King did not criticize Carmichael in public, in private he tried to persuade him to tone down his remarks. Carmichael only became bolder. At one point, he declared, "This country don't run on love, brother. It's run on power, and we ain't got none!"

Carmichael's heated statements captured the attention of the media. He replaced King in the headlines and alienated many of the SCLC's white and middle-class black supporters. To them, Black Power was a new form of racism directed at whites.

Stokely Carmichael (1941–1998) and the Black Panthers

Stokely Carmichael was born in Trinidad in 1941. At the age of eleven, he moved with his family to New York City and became a U.S. citizen. Carmichael attended Howard University in Washington, D.C., where he staged protests against segregation in the nation's capital. He also participated in the Freedom Rides and the civil rights demonstrations in Albany, Georgia.

After graduating from Howard, Carmichael joined the staff of SNCC. Two years later, he replaced the moderate John Lewis as the organization's national chairman.

Stokely Carmichael left SNCC in 1967 and became honorary prime minister of the Black Panther Party for Self-Defense. Many SNCC members followed him into this new and more **militant** organization. Although the Black Panthers sponsored a few worthwhile projects, such as a breakfast program for poor children, they were also involved in drug dealing, robbery, assault, and murder. Many of the Black Panthers eventually went to prison for their crimes.

Carmichael later moved to Africa, settled in Guinea, and changed his name to Kwame Ture. He died in Guinea in 1998.

Stokely Carmichael giving a speech in 1970. Carmichael eventually left the United States and became active in the African Liberation Movement. The movement aimed to free the countries of Africa from colonial rule and restore their native culture.

De Facto Segregation

After his successful struggle against legal segregation, King turned his attention to de facto segregation—the kind of racism that existed in fact and was practiced and accepted almost universally in the North. The most glaring example of de facto segregation could be found in the housing patterns that kept African Americans living in ghettos and confined their children to all-black schools. Combined with this was a general indifference to the fact that blacks were regularly barred from first-class restaurants, private schools, and social clubs, and generally held low-level jobs such as janitors or maids.

> . . . King turned his attention to de facto segregation—the kind of racism that existed in fact and was practiced and accepted almost universally in the North.

Early in 1966, King began organizing the Chicago Freedom Movement (CFM). The city had close to a million blacks, but the people involved in local real estate—including bankers, builders, and real estate brokers—with the cooperation of Chicago's politicians, had devised a system of rules and regulations that prevented blacks from moving into any white neighborhoods.

Real estate brokers would only show homes to blacks in black neighborhoods. If blacks managed to find homes elsewhere, banks would refuse their applications for mortgages. It was also common for homeowners to sign legal documents, called restrictive covenants, in which they pledged not to sell their property to certain ethnic groups, usually blacks and Jews. The CFM's goal was to abolish these practices and secure the adoption of an open-housing law that would allow blacks to live wherever they pleased.

In an effort to gain equal housing rights, protestors conduct a rally at Chicago's Soldier Field in July 1966. King then led the demonstrators to City Hall.

In July, King addressed a rally in Soldier Field in downtown Chicago. Afterward, he led a march of more than ten thousand people to City Hall to demand an end to discrimination in the sale and rental of homes. King soon found out that Chicago's whites were violently opposed to open housing. He also did not get the cooperation he expected from the city's blacks. Many of them were hostile to whites and did not want to negotiate with them. They also had no respect for ministers and were not interested in moral crusades.

Chicago's mayor, Richard Daley, treated King politely and made a show of responding to his demands, but the CFM ended with nothing but vague promises. In the spring of 1966, President Lyndon B. Johnson had sent a third civil rights bill to Congress. Its main provision was a ban on discrimination in housing. King had hoped that the Chicago Freedom Movement would hasten its passage. But in September, the bill died on the floor of the Senate. The Senate majority leader, Mike Mansfield of Montana, blamed extremists on both sides of the civil rights struggle for its failure. Although Mansfield did not mention Stokely Carmichael by name, he left little doubt that Carmichael's harsh criticism of the bill as being too weak had irritated many senators and prompted them to vote against it.

A New Direction

In the summer of 1966, a year after Watts, there were riots in the slums of some two dozen Northern cities. The death and destruction they caused dealt a fatal blow to the civil rights movement. Even whites who were sympathetic to blacks wanted no part of such lawless behavior. Middle-class blacks were equally horrified. The country's interest in racial issues declined, and people turned their attention to other matters.

Although the riots left King depressed, they did not dampen his desire to help America's blacks. In November 1967, he told his aides that it was time to open the "second phase" of the

Although the riots left King depressed, they did not dampen his desire to help America's blacks.

civil rights struggle—the Poor People's Campaign. The new campaign would use direct nonviolent action to eliminate poverty. It would be an enormous undertaking aimed at helping not only blacks but other disadvantaged minorities such as Native Americans, Latinos, and poor whites.

In announcing the new campaign, King said, "It required a Selma before the fundamental right to vote was written into the federal statutes. It took a Birmingham before the government moved to open doors of public accommodations to all human beings. What we need now is a new kind of Selma or Birmingham to dramatize the economic plight of the Negro and compel the government to act."

Members of the Poor People's Campaign marching through downtown Washington on June 18, 1968. The demonstrators stayed in tents and shacks set up along the Mall and caused so many problems that the city breathed a sigh of relief when they left.

The Poor People's Campaign would be modeled on the 1963 March on Washington. Instead of a one-day demonstration, however, the participants would stay in the capital, camping on the Mall, until the federal government met their demand for a $30 billion anti-poverty program. The campaign was to begin in April 1968.

Several of King's aides pointed out that the SCLC did not have enough staff members to organize a project as ambitious as the Poor People's Campaign. Some of them doubted that it would succeed. In February, with the campaign only weeks away, they asked him to postpone the demonstration until they could hire more people and make sure the event did not dissolve into chaos. King listened to their concerns, but he thought their worries were groundless. The Poor People's Campaign would take place as planned.

CHAPTER 13

Free at Last

I may not get there with you, but I want you to know tonight that we, as a people, will get to the Promised Land.

While Martin Luther King, Jr., was working on the plans for his Poor People's Campaign, he received a call from the Reverend James Lawson. As a divinity student, Lawson had counseled some of the students who founded SNCC. Now he was the pastor of a black church in Memphis, Tennessee.

Some weeks earlier, Memphis's sanitation workers—a nearly all-black workforce—had gone on strike. They were demanding safer working conditions, an increase in pay, and recognition of their labor union. The city's black community was supporting the workers with marches and mass meetings, but the strike remained unsettled. Lawson wanted King to speak at a rally for the strikers.

With the Poor People's Campaign still in a state of confusion, King could not spare the time to visit Memphis. Nevertheless, he was intrigued by Lawson's invitation. The sanitation workers' strike was a perfect example of the link between race and poverty. Because the workers were black, they could get only low-paying jobs with little or no security. This was the point King wanted to make in his Poor People's Campaign. Memphis would serve as a preview of the campaign. King told Lawson he would come to the city for a single speech on March 18.

The Memphis March

On the appointed evening, some fifteen thousand people crowded into Memphis's Mason Temple. King was so carried away by the warm reception they gave him that he promised to return on March 22 and lead a march in support of the sanitation workers. King's aides begged him to change his mind. Large marches required extensive planning. Four days would not give them enough time to make adequate preparations.

King was so carried away by the warm reception they gave him that he promised to return on March 22 . . .

King brushed aside their objections. The vitality and sense of purpose he had seen in Memphis reminded him of the early years of the civil rights movement. He could not resist the chance to recapture those heady days before riots and cries for black power had sapped the movement's strength.

On March 22, Memphis was experiencing one of its infrequent snowstorms. The march was put off until March 28. King's flight into Memphis that day was late, so the march was delayed until he arrived. While the marchers were waiting, the members of a youth gang called the Invaders began heckling a crowd of teenagers stationed at the end of the line. The Invaders were associated with a militant black organization that had been excluded from the parade. They taunted the teenagers for marching when they ought to be causing some real trouble.

James Lawson and the volunteers who were supervising the march had positioned themselves at the head of the line. They could not see the wine bottles that were being passed around among the young people at the rear. By the time King arrived and the march began, the teenagers were out of control. A few

The day after the March 28, 1968, riot in Memphis, the sanitation workers held a second march. This time, the Tennessee National Guard was on hand to keep order. The strikers wore "I <u>AM</u> A MAN" signs to remind people of their dignity as human beings.

minutes later, the sound of breaking glass was heard. Egged on by the Invaders, the young marchers were smashing store windows and looting their contents. Other marchers joined them, shouting, "Black Power!" and "Burn it, baby!"

As police officers rushed to put down the riot, King's aides hailed a passing motorist, who drove him to a safer part of the city. Before the riot ended, sixty-two people had been injured and a black teenager was dead. Many people held King responsible for the disorder. A *New York Times* editorial advised him to call off the Poor People's Campaign to avoid "another eruption of the kind that rocked Memphis."

King considered taking the newspaper's advice. At the same time, he felt compelled to prove that civil rights demonstrations could still be conducted in an orderly way. He announced that he would return to Memphis and lead another march on April 5. This one would be totally free of violence. To make sure that it was, King would bring along some of his aides and not rely on local volunteers.

King's Assassination

King arrived in Memphis on April 3. He and his aides checked into the Lorraine Motel in a black section of the city. A bomb threat had delayed King's flight from Atlanta. Although no bomb was found, the threat left King with thoughts of death.

In his speech that evening, he said, "Like anybody, I would like to live a long life. Longevity has its place. But I'm not concerned about that now. I just want to do God's will. And he's allowed me to go up to the mountain. And I've looked over. And I've seen the Promised Land. I may not get there with you, but I want you to know tonight that we, as a people, will get to the Promised Land."

> In his speech that evening, he said, "Like anybody, I would like to live a long life . . . But I'm not concerned about that now. I just want to do God's will."

The city of Memphis had applied for an injunction to ban the march. King and his aides spent the next day, April 4, at the Lorraine Motel waiting to hear the judge's decision. Late that afternoon, an SCLC lawyer appeared with word that the judge had agreed to let the march proceed. The news put everyone in a good mood.

Martin Luther King, Jr., walking across the balcony of the Lorraine Motel shortly after his arrival in Memphis on April 3, 1968. He was killed the next evening in approximately the same spot.

King and his aides were invited to dinner that night at the home of a Memphis minister. While they were getting ready to leave, King stepped out on the balcony of the room he shared with Ralph Abernathy. Suddenly, a shot echoed through the motel courtyard. A bullet struck King in the neck. Abernathy ran out and found his friend lying on the balcony, bleeding and unconscious. King was rushed to the hospital, but there was nothing the doctors could do. He was pronounced dead at 7:05 p.m. He was thirty-nine years old.

Within hours of Martin Luther King, Jr.'s assassination, the FBI identified his killer. He was a white man named James Earl Ray, who had recently escaped from the Missouri State Penitentiary. Ray had read in a newspaper where King would be staying and had rented a room in a seedy rooming house across the way. His fingerprints were found on the rifle and binoculars he had left behind when he fled.

The wanted poster of James Earl Ray. He was taken into custody in London on June 8 while trying to enter Great Britain. He confessed to the killing of Martin Luther King, Jr., but later claimed that a man he knew only as "Raoul" had done it.

Ray was taken into custody two months later. He confessed to the killing and received a sentence of ninety-nine years in prison. Many people—including members of King's family—believe that Ray did not act alone, but no evidence of a **conspiracy** was ever found. Ray died in prison in 1998.

The Reaction to King's Death

Despite the fact that President Lyndon B. Johnson had declared a national day of mourning, the news of Martin Luther King, Jr.'s death set off riots in Chicago, Baltimore, Washington, D.C., Detroit, and over a hundred other cities across the country. They lasted for the next three weeks. President Lyndon B. Johnson dispatched some fifty thousand U.S. Army troops and National Guardsmen to curb the violence and restore order. By the time the riots ended, forty-six people had been killed and over two thousand injured.

King's coffin was carried through the streets of Atlanta on a farm wagon pulled by a team of Georgia mules—a symbol of King's identification with poor people. The funeral service was held at Ebenezer Baptist Church. Vice President Hubert H. Humphrey represented President Lyndon B. Johnson. Former Vice President Richard M. Nixon, John F. Kennedy's widow, Jacqueline, and his brother Robert, now a senator from New York, were also among those present. The other guests included representatives from all the major religious faiths and the mayors of most of the nation's big cities.

At Coretta Scott King's request, the services included a tape of her husband's last sermon at Ebenezer Baptist Church, which he had preached on February 4. The church service was followed by a second service at Morehouse College, where his old friend, Dr. Benjamin Mays, gave the eulogy.

Robert F. Kennedy's Speech

In the spring of 1968, Robert F. Kennedy was campaigning for the Democratic nomination for president. He arrived in Indianapolis, Indiana, on the evening of April 4 and was informed of King's assassination. Kennedy was scheduled to make a speech in the city's black ghetto that evening, but the police advised him against it. Kennedy decided to speak anyway. When he arrived at the site, he realized that the crowd was not aware of King's death. He would have to break the news to them.

Speaking without any notes, Kennedy told the crowd what had happened in Memphis. He urged them to follow King's teachings on nonviolence and respond to his death with understanding and prayers. Kennedy entreated them to avoid division, hatred, and violence and stressed the need for love, wisdom, compassion, and justice.

Thanks to Kennedy's speech, Indianapolis was the only major city in the country where there were no riots.

Following the assassination of Martin Luther King, Jr., Attorney General Robert F. Kennedy, shown in this 1964 photograph, addressed a crowd in Indianapolis, Indiana. He broke the news of King's death to them in an eloquent and compassionate speech.

King's family and friends attending his funeral at Ebenezer Baptist Church. Ralph Abernathy, the first speaker at the service, called King's murder "one of the darkest hours of mankind." Jesse Jackson (far right) was among the mourners.

King was originally buried beside his maternal grandparents in Atlanta's Southview Cemetery. His body was later moved to a site near Ebenezer Baptist Church. The words on his tombstone are taken from a Negro spiritual: "Free at last, Thank God Almighty I'm free at last."

The words on his tombstone are taken from a Negro spiritual: "Free at last, Thank God Almighty I'm free at last."

Life After King

After King's death, the civil rights movement, which was already in decline, drifted into disarray. Ralph Abernathy became head of the SCLC but he lacked King's gift for leadership. Although the Poor People's Campaign took place as planned, it was badly organized and ended up a failure. The civil rights movement faded into history, as most movements do, but it had a lasting impact on the country.

After her husband's death, Coretta Scott King continued his work. Shown here at the 1976 Democratic Convention in New York City—where Jimmy Carter received his party's nomination for president—she and Carter led the delegates in singing "We Shall Overcome."

As a widow, Coretta Scott King dedicated her life to carrying on her husband's work. Within days of his funeral, she led a march on behalf of the Memphis sanitation workers. Later that month, she appeared in his place at an anti-Vietnam War rally in New York. In June, she spoke at the Lincoln Memorial in Washington during the opening of the Poor People's Campaign.

In 1969, Coretta published her autobiography, *My Life with Martin Luther King, Jr.* She served on the boards of directors of the Southern Christian Leadership Conference and the National Organization for Women. When a national holiday was established in her husband's honor, she became chairperson of the Martin Luther King, Jr. Federal Holiday Commission. The commission was created by an Act of Congress and charged with drawing up plans for the annual celebration, which began in 1986.

As a tribute to Martin Luther King, Jr., Coretta Scott King also established The King Center in Atlanta. The complex contains an exhibition hall, conference facilities, a research library, and the marble crypt in which King was interred after his body was moved from South View Cemetery. The King Center is part of Atlanta's Martin Luther King, Jr. National Historic Site, which also includes Ebenezer Baptist Church and King's childhood home on Auburn Avenue.

Martin Luther King, Jr.'s, Legacy

A few days after Martin Luther King, Jr., was killed, President Johnson signed the Civil Rights Act of 1968 into law. The bill, which is known as the Fair Housing Act, prohibits discrimination in the sale, rental, and financing of housing. In Memphis, the sanitation workers won an increase in wages, and the city agreed to recognize their labor union.

A National Holiday

Four days after Martin Luther King, Jr.'s assassination, Representative John Conyers of Michigan introduced a bill to create a federal holiday in his honor. The bill was not passed, but Conyers and another African American representative, Shirley Chisholm, of New York, continued to introduce it at every session of Congress for the next fifteen years. It was finally passed in 1983. President Ronald Reagan signed it into law. The holiday is celebrated on the third Monday in January, a date that is close to King's birthday on January 15.

On November 2, 1983, President Ronald Reagan signed the bill that established a federal holiday in honor of Martin Luther King, Jr. Coretta is shown attending the signing, which took place in the White House Rose Garden.

In the years between 1955, when the Montgomery bus boycott began, and 1965, when the Voting Rights Act was passed, African Americans made significant progress in their struggle for political, social, and economic equality.

In addition to securing the passage of federal civil rights laws, the movement fostered the talents of young African Americans who later found places in the larger political world. One of King's aides, Andrew Young, was elected to Congress and later served as ambassador to the United Nations and mayor of

Atlanta. Another, Jesse Jackson, became a political activist and a serious, though unsuccessful, candidate for president. John Lewis, former national chairman of SNCC, has been a congressman in Georgia since 1987.

The struggle is far from over. Hate speech persists. Slights and slurs are not uncommon. Disagreements over **affirmative action**, school segregation, and discrimination in employment and housing continue to find their way into the courts. Racial prejudice may never be completely wiped out, but Martin Luther King brought the nation a giant step closer to tolerance. Thanks to his courage and perseverance, a gross injustice was finally rectified. The United States Constitution is no longer a white-only document. Its words apply to all Americans regardless of the color of their skin.

. . . African Americans made significant progress in their struggle for political, social, and economic equality.

This postage stamp honoring Martin Luther King, Jr., went on sale in Atlanta, Georgia, on January 13, 1979, two days before the fiftieth anniversary of his birth. The stamp carries a portrait of King along with a picture of one of his famous marches.

Glossary

affirmative action—a policy or program for correcting the effects of discrimination in the employment or education of certain groups, such as blacks or women.

amendments—revisions or changes in a law.

Anglican—a member of the Church of England.

bail—money deposited with a court to get an arrested person released on the promise that he or she will return for trial.

bigot—a person who holds strong prejudices against people of different races, religions, or political views.

boycott—a joining together in refusal to deal with a businessperson, company, organization, or nation.

civil disobedience—the refusal to obey a law or follow a policy that is considered unjust.

concessions—rights or privileges that are granted to settle a dispute.

conspiracy—an agreement to act together in planning an illegal, treacherous, or evil deed.

constitution—the document containing the fundamental laws and principles of a government.

dilemma—a situation that requires a person to choose between two equally bad, or good, alternatives.

dissertation—a lengthy paper on a scholarly subject that is among the requirements for receiving an advanced degree.

doctorate—a Doctor of Philosophy (PhD), the highest academic degree granted by a university.

fasts—eating little or no food for a prolonged period.

federal marshals—the men and women who enforce federal laws and protect federal courts, witnesses, and prisoners.

injunction—a court order requiring or forbidding a particular action.

integration—the removal of the legal and social barriers preventing the races from associating with each other.

lynching—to kill a person by mob action without a lawful trial. Hanging was the most common method of lynching.

militant—to be aggressive, especially in the service of a cause.

minstrel shows—variety shows presented by performers in "blackface" (theatrical makeup), who sing, dance, and tell jokes.

municipal—involving a city or its government.

oratorical—having to do with public speaking.

philosophy—the study of the laws and ideas that affect human thought and conduct.

segregation—the separation of the races imposed by law or custom.

sit-ins—sit-downs in public places by groups of people protesting a particular policy or action.

stalemate—a situation in which further action is impossible.

strikes—suspensions of normal activity undertaken as protests against those in power.

valedictory—a farewell speech delivered at a school graduation.

white supremacists—those who believe that whites are superior to people of other races.

Bibliography

Branch, Taylor. *At Canaan's Edge: America in the King Years, 1965-68*. New York: Simon & Schuster, 2006.

Branch, Taylor. *Parting the Waters: America in the King Years, 1954-63*. New York: Simon & Schuster, 1988.

Branch, Taylor. *Pillar of Fire: America in the King Years, 1963-65*. New York: Simon & Schuster, 1998.

Frady, Marshall. *Martin Luther King, Jr.* New York: The Penguin Group, 2002.

King, Coretta Scott. *My Life with Martin Luther King, Jr.* New York: Henry Holt & Co., 1969.

McWhorter, Diane. *A Dream of Freedom: The Civil Rights Movement from 1954 to 1968*. New York: Scholastic Inc., 2004.

Miller, William Robert. *Martin Luther King, Jr.: His Life, Martyrdom, and Meaning for the World*. New York: Weybright and Talley, 1968.

Oates, Stephen B. *Let the Trumpet Sound: The Life of Martin Luther King, Jr.* New York: Harper & Row Publishers, 1982.

Rubel, David. *The Coming Free: The Struggle for African-American Equality*. New York, DK Publishing, 2005.

Washington, James M. (editor). *A Testament of Hope: The Essential Writings and Speeches of Martin Luther King, Jr.* New York: Harper & Row, Publishers, 1986.

Williams, Juan. *Eyes on the Prize: America's Civil Rights Years, 1954-1965*. New York: The Penguin Group, 1988.

The Martin Luther King, Jr. Companion: Quotations from the Speeches, Essays, and Books of Martin Luther King, Jr. Selected by Coretta Scott King. New York: St. Martin's Press, 1993.

Image Credits

About the Author

Alice Fleming has written more than thirty books for adults and young people. Her interest in American history has led her to write biographies of such famous Americans as George Washington, Frederick Douglass, P. T. Barnum, Ida Tarbell, and Senator Margaret Chase Smith. Ms. Fleming lives in New York City with her husband, novelist and historian Thomas Fleming.

Index